BEACONS

BEACONS
Great Teachers of the Georgetown School of Foreign Service

Edited by
MARGERY BOICHEL THOMPSON

Foreword by
PETER F. KROGH

Edmund A. Walsh School of Foreign Service
Georgetown University

75 YEARS: CHARTING THE HORIZON OF INTERNATIONAL EDUCATION

GEORGETOWN UNIVERSITY
Edmund A. Walsh School of Foreign Service
Washington, DC 20057

© 1994, Edmund A. Walsh School of Foreign Service,
Georgetown University

All rights reserved.
Printed in the United States of America

LIBRARY OF CONGRESS CATALOGING-IN-PUBLICATION DATA

Beacons : great teachers of the Georgetown School of Foreign Service /
edited by Margery Boichel Thompson ; foreword by Peter F. Krogh.
    p.   cm.
    Includes bibliographical references.
    ISBN 0-934742-77-4
    1. World politics—20th century .   2. World politics—to 1900 .
I. Boichel , Margery R.   II. Georgetown University. School of
Foreign Service.
D840 . B38   1994
327 \ . 09 \ 04—dc20   94-32604
                                                    CIP

Contents

CHAPTER		PAGE
	Peter F. Krogh Foreword	vii
	Acknowledgments	ix
1	Edmund A. Walsh, S.J. See Life Steadily and See It Whole	1
2	Frank L. Fadner, S.J. Russia's Jesuit Province of COLLEGIUM GEORGEOPOLITANUM	9
3	Carroll Quigley The State of Individuals, 1776–1976	21
4	Jan Karski War and Peace in Soviet Diplomacy, 1939	47
5	Joseph S. Sebes, S.J. Vietnam: Civil War or War of Aggression?	73
6	Jules Davids A World in Turmoil	93
7	Walter I. Giles The Constitutional Right to Privacy: From GRISWOLD to ROE V. WADE and Beyond	117
8	Joseph Zrinyi, S.J. "Passive Agent of Omnipotent Capital": The Entrepreneur in Marxian Theory	127
9	George J. Viksnins Joseph Schumpeter Revisited	141
10	William V. O'Brien Scholarship on the Laws of War: Some Reflections	153
11	Madeleine Albright Strategic Vision for the 1990s: Moving beyond Containment	173
	About the Authors	185

Foreword

Peter F. Krogh
Dean, Georgetown School of Foreign Service

All great educational institutions ultimately rest on the shoulders of great teachers. Put another way, a great school is a composite of the extended shadows of its master teachers. Nowhere has this been more true than at the Edmund A. Walsh School of Foreign Service.

The requirement of excellent teaching was articulated and represented by the School's founder, Edmund A. Walsh, S.J. To launch the School he assembled outstanding teacher-scholars and teacher-practitioners and set the tone himself as the School's preeminent lecturer. Appropriately and eloquently, an address by Father Walsh illuminating his humanistic ideas on education for international relations leads off this volume.

Father Walsh's example was embraced, embellished, and embroidered by a succession of great teachers drawn from within and without the Jesuit order. A representative sampling is offered here, including selections by Father Frank Fadner and Father Joe Sebes, who, while devotedly investing themselves in teaching and counseling, both served terms as regents of the School, Father Sebes also as dean.

Giants also are numbered among the School's lay faculty, led by the redoubtable Carroll Quigley and followed closely by Jack Giles, Jules Davids, and Bill O'Brien. Professors Quigley and Giles have been singled out by this country's current president as having been instrumental in his formation; Professor Davids assisted an earlier president (then senator), John F. Kennedy, on his prize-winning *Profiles in Courage;* and Professor O'Brien was the intellectual father of the School's current undergraduate curriculum.

Historically the School and the university at large have benefited, disproportionately to their numbers, from distinguished Central European intellectuals. Prominent among these in the School's classrooms have been (in addition to Father Sebes) Jan Karski, Father Joseph Zrinyi, and George Viksnins. Their personal qualities and the style and substance of their lectures are indelibly etched in the minds of generations of students.

This volume concludes with a presentation by Madeleine Albright. Before taking leave to serve as U.S. ambassador to the United Nations, she had won the School's outstanding undergraduate teaching award in five consecutive years.

The selections presented here are drawn not only from teachers who figure prominently in the School's history but from fields of study—international affairs, world and diplomatic history, government, law, and economics—that have figured prominently in the School's educational program. Perforce the volume excludes a legion of outstanding SFS teachers equally deserving of inclusion. Suffice it to say that this volume is equally—and gratefully—a tribute to them.

The School of Foreign Service teaching program seeks to provide a compass to help guide the life journey of its graduates as they pursue their exploration of the world in all its dimensions and quarters. Those who taught them here serve them there as beacons.

Acknowledgments

Several people have helped greatly in the shaping and production of this book: Dr. Peter F. Krogh, dean of the Georgetown School of Foreign Service, generously contributed the book's foreword. It was Dean Krogh also who conceived the idea of gathering into a book a representative sampling of the School's renowned and well-remembered teachers as an indispensable component of its seventy-fifth anniversary celebrations.

Others on the faculty and staff of the School provided invaluable assistance: Professors Francis X. Winters, S.J., and David S. Painter lent their expertise by vetting two of the book's chapters; Professor George Viksnins and Father Winters provided vital bits of color on individual authors not known by the editor; university archivist Jon Reynolds and the Lauinger Special Collections staff helped in the search for writings and photographs; Gail Griffith coordinated elements of the book's production and came up with two of its chapters; and Mireia Villar Forner and Greg A. Caires helped immeasurably in the preparation of the manuscript. Thanks are due also to Professors Giles, Karski, O'Brien, and Viksnins, Ambassador Albright, and Frances Davids, on behalf of Professor Davids, for their cooperation on their chapters; to the GU Office of Publications for the classic SFS cover; and to Irene Petrlik, director of Concept, for the book's striking text design and composition.

Margery Boichel Thompson

CHAPTER 1

See Life Steadily and See It Whole

EDMUND A. WALSH, S.J.

On May 11, 1934, the founder and regent of the Georgetown School of Foreign Service, Edmund A. Walsh, S.J., addressed a conference at the University of Delaware on the role of the American college in international relations. Father Walsh recognized the new demands created by fundamental changes in the international scene and chose as his theme the idea that "one must see life steadily and see it whole," as Matthew Arnold phrased it when characterizing Greek philosophy. Clearly visible in these remarks—and in the works of other notable faculty in this volume—was the philosophy guiding Father Walsh's pioneering leadership of the School of Foreign Service.

SOURCE: *Footnotes to History: Selected Speeches and Writings of Edmund A. Walsh, S.J.*, ed. Anna Watkins (Washington, D.C.: Georgetown University Press, 1990), pp. 73–81.

See Life Steadily and See It Whole

It would doubtless be a twice-told tale in such an assembly as this to enumerate the changes in substance and methods of teaching that have been introduced into education and university perspectives by the historic events of the last twenty years [1914–1934]. It is no exaggeration to say that the heavy responsibilities devolving so suddenly on the United States, as an aftermath of that collective insanity called the World War, created national and governmental obligations for which our people as a whole were intellectually and psychologically unprepared. Dislodged from isolated ease and uprooted from our parochial complacency, we were bidden to think and act internationally.

What frequently happens in unforeseen emergencies actually happened to our postwar mentality. Improvisation followed fast on the heels of enlarged responsibility. Increasing commitments inevitably followed increased participation in world affairs. Alluring vistas of international service opened up to challenge a nation that previously had been concerned with the tremendous task of solving specific domestic problems, caused partly by the Civil War and partly by the ever-increasing industrialization of American society. To be sure, international law and foreign relations had long occupied the attention of scholars and experts, but had left the broad masses of the people untouched and unaffected. The Spanish-American War, with its concomitant widening of territorial jurisdiction, was only a prelude and a warning of the subsequent phase that swept us, for a decade after the Armistice, into a complexity of international relations that needs no rehearsal here.

Educators were not slow to recognize their obligations to the new destiny confronting America; interest in foreign affairs and training for a worthy participation in the Golden Age that was

Edmund A. Walsh, S.J.

to ensue received powerful and widespread stimulus in academic circles. To assist in mobilizing the constructive thoughts and information that should serve as the mainspring for giving direction to national policy was the motive underlying the creation in February 1919 of the School of Foreign Service of Georgetown University. International peace through international understanding then was, and still is, the school's rule of conduct.

There are two notions in that expression of purpose, namely, peace and order. These are terms that need defining lest the declared objective be obscured by fascinating but irrelevant and dangerous accidentals, which take the form of special interests, unattainable ideals, laborious technical instrumentalities, and emotional exaggerations. The art of the possible in the conduct of international relations is the most realistic definition of diplomacy I have discovered, for it accepts that stern discipline which the facts of history impose on thoughtful people. It reminds the enthusiast and confirms for the cautious that international relations are phenomena conducted by human beings among human beings, not by archangels among disembodied spirits devoid of human passion, free of prejudice, unfettered by racial or national tradition, and superior to the other intangibles that so profoundly modify theory and practice.

Peace, then, like all problems whether practical or speculative, should first be defined. *Ignoti nulla cupido*, runs the wise Latin proverb, there is no desire for the unknown thing. Hence peace begins in the intellect, not primarily in the will, which is the principle of external operation. The best definition of peace I know is "the tranquility of order." For where disorder exists, whether in the mental processes or in the moral life of individuals and communities, there is no tranquility of mind. Conversely, where order rules the intellect and will, satisfaction—which is only another term for tranquility—ensues.

International peace, therefore, will result from a satisfactory ordering of rights, obligations, and mutual conduct. We hear much about the rights attaching to nationhood; but we hear

See Life Steadily and See It Whole

less about the obligations resulting from membership in the great family of nations. Yet these are correlative terms, and the sovereign rights of one people are the obligations of all others in respect to the possessor.

Order is defined as *apta dispositio plurium ad unum*, the right arrangement of many objects in order to achieve unity of purpose. The chairs in a room are for the use of its occupants and hence are placed in convenient locations on the floor where people may sit on them; they are not suspended from the ceiling, out of reach. And the postprandial tranquility of a giant beast of prey derives from his having swallowed some weaker animal; that is his idea of the right order of things.

If, then, international order implies some controlling goal or objective, it is clear that the effect to be achieved must be independent of and superior to the subjective whims, political ambitions, and prejudices of the widely divergent units that make up this world family of approximately two billion restless human beings—assuming, that is, that they wish to live in the social intercourse characteristic of society as organized today. The gunfire of an irresponsible youth at Sarajevo, in the summer of 1914, proved how interdependent nations are and how sensitive the nerves of the social organisms have become.

The next deduction is inescapable. Were peace committed to the uncontrolled and arbitrary interpretation of half a hundred individual governments, the antagonisms and clashing of national ambitions and racial prejudices would conspire to produce not order, but chaos. Economic "laissez-faire" and the extreme individualism of the Manchester School have reduced our generation to the present industrial disorder. Similarly, political "laissez-faire" on an international scale, resulting in an unreasonable chauvinism, brought Western civilization to the brink of the precipice in 1914. I do not see how we can long escape a similar dilemma, followed by a more appalling tragedy, unless the nations agree on a principle of fundamental spiritual and moral control.

This principle must be universally applicable, purged of the vicious cynicism of Machiavelli's *Prince*, and capable of profoundly moving the depths of man's cultural nature when le-

Edmund A. Walsh, S.J.

galities leave him cold and skeptical. The only standard that can meet these requirements is an awakened sense of international justice, international respect, and mutual toleration. The alternative is the rule of force and a return to the ethics of the jungle. Should an unrelieved and stubborn nationalism become the controlling norm of conduct, I see for the future only a reversion to the narrow localism prevalent in the age of feudalism. Governments and peoples would withdraw behind guarded ramparts, there to devote their energies to the primitive appetites of self-preservation, self-protection, self-sufficiency, and selfish national aggrandizement. A glacial cap would settle over civilization and the ice age of international relations would return. So long as the League of Nations, as constituted at the present time, perpetuates the domination of the so-called major powers in the Council over the lesser in the Assembly, it will, in my opinion, be helpless before the steady drift of elemental human forces.

Justice must always extend her jurisdiction from the municipal to the international circuit. Justice in the last analysis simply means rendering to each what is clearly his, *unicuique suum*. There is no infallible public tribunal to resolve that vexed question and to preserve moral equilibrium among men, as we have again learned during the past few years, this time from the Far East. The instinct for justice must be cultivated from below; the seeds must be planted in the hearts, the minds, and the wills of men; it cannot be expected to bloom automatically at the top of the social structure, if it has not roots in the understanding of the people.

It is the unending function, then, of education and the spiritual forces of the world to defend this moral substitute for war. It is the responsibility of the independent thinkers of humanity to interpret the appeal of reason and to refuse to be intellectually debauched by fear of the consequences, by political or party considerations, or by the curling lip of professional propagandists.

In a sense, there is no such thing among states as absolute

See Life Steadily and See It Whole

sovereignty. But there is such a thing as sovereign equality, whether possessed by Russia or Geneva, as John Marshall phrased it. So long as man is destined by nature to live in the society of his fellow men, all his rights have a social as well as an individual aspect and no right can be so exercised as to positively injure the common good of the whole community. The sovereign rights of the smallest republic are the reciprocal obligations of the most formidable empire.

Let us be realists without ceasing to be idealists and learn something from the lessons of the past two decades. If hopes for international peace are now at the lowest ebb conceivable, may the disillusionment not be due to the exalted plane to which aspiration was artificially elevated? I am no cynic nor skeptic when I say that one of the most effective enemies to international peace is the opinionated, exaggerated zealot who promises the millennium at the close of his little day. The long record of human nature spread before me forbids me to entertain the hope, however inspirational, that man will leap across centuries, rather than progress by slow toilsome labor, to higher levels of civilized living.

Much has been successfully done, particularly in the way of arousing a popular consciousness of the problem, but much remains for the undisclosed future. I for one am far from being discouraged. I know that Christianity, after nineteen centuries, fortified with a divine mandate as it was, and interpreted by the finest minds and voices, has succeeded in persuading only one-third of the human race to accept the new dispensation! It would be the ecstasy of hysteria and the very definition of conceit for us to expect better results within the brief space of one generation.

There is a clear responsibility, therefore, resting both on the students of international relations and the university which undertakes to prepare them for that chosen field. Among those obligations I should count frankness among the first, and honesty, and the ability to see life steadily and see it whole. Technical and specialized information is of the highest importance but becomes wholly inadequate unless humanized

Edmund A. Walsh, S.J.

by a broad and liberal background, which alone can insure the intelligent and fruitful application of factual knowledge to human relations.

I have long been of the opinion that peace propaganda, in common with democracy and capitalism, must undergo serious revision of its methods. While thoroughly persuaded of the continuing necessity of international peace through international understanding, I am more than ever convinced that the soundest basis on which to build international peace is a tolerant and enlightened nationalism that accepts the historic reality that few governments have ever been known to confer an unadulterated and purely disinterested favor on another. The opposite contention is a delusion which only time will cure. An emotional and uninformed internationalism may well become as dangerous through lack of proportion as the most bumptious and belligerent nationalism.

If ever cool heads and steady hands were needed at the helms of the ships of state and in the public forum which universities provide, it is at the present hour; otherwise the peace of the world lies at the mercy of an accident. Another war, particularly in the prevailing environment of disturbed social conditions and widespread popular discontent, would be suicide as well as homicide for the government deliberately provoking it. And the infection would spread. . . . That would mean either an extension of communism or the gradual increase of dictatorships in one form or another. The return of more Caesars cannot but weaken the claims of democracy.

I do not suggest that we have, or ever did have, a mandate to make the world safe for democracy. Woodrow Wilson inverted the order of nature; he should have first made democracy safe for the world. The universities and colleges of the land, as never before, are on notice that they will be expected to meet the test by furnishing responsible information, temperate judgments, and impartial scholarship. The time has come to devote more attention to the production of leaders than to leadership in production.

CHAPTER 2

Russia's Jesuit Province of Collegium Georgeopolitanum

Frank L. Fadner, S.J.

> Expert in Russian history, exceptional polylinguist, and accomplished artist, Father Fadner taught history at Georgetown from 1949 to 1978 and also served as the School of Foreign Service regent. He is remembered in his later years as a magnificent figure with a full beard and flashing eyes, sporting a walking stick and an unusual hat. The fascinating story he tells here links the Russian saga in the "vicissitudes of the Jesuits" with the early survival of Georgetown University. Originally delivered as a lecture to the Georgetown Institute of Languages and Linguistics Anniversary Series "Russia: Thought and Spirit," it was published in the *Georgetown Magazine* Winter 1965 edition.

Russia's Jesuit Province of COLLEGIUM GEORGEOPOLITANUM

An eminent scholar, Rev. John M. Daley, S.J., has noted that the "history of the restoration of the Society of Jesus in the United States and the history of Georgetown College are intimately connected." A third factor in the story is the minor Jesuit theme in history's Great Russian symphony, for there have been Russian highlights in the tale of the vicissitudes of the Jesuits.

The catalogue of events and happenstances in this regard is a lengthy one. The Russia of Ivan the Terrible was the setting for the activities of the Jesuit diplomat Antonio Possevino, who was sent by Gregory XIII to bring about the union of the Greek and Latin churches. The Latin West's reaction to the establishment of a Russian national Patriarchate was reflected in the inauguration of the Uniate at Brest in 1595. In the years following, a naive and bitter Moscow was to look upon the Uniate as a Polish and Jesuit-inspired plot to foment schism and unrest among the people of the so-called "Western Russian lands" and to alienate them from Moscow.

Within a decade Muscovite Russia was to lie prostrate during the terrible Time of Troubles—eight years of an awful civil war, which Russians were to feel they owed to the intrigues of Jesuits who supported the first False Dmitrii and the Polish invasion of Russia, capped by two years of the rule of a Polish tsar in Holy Moscow.

Symbolic of this Muscovite tradition, of course, is the role assigned, and the melancholy fate meted out, to the Jesuits Rangoni, Lavitskii, and Chernykovskii in the great folk drama *Boris Godunov*. Typical, too, was the ringing slogan of the Hetman, Bogdan Khmelnitskii, as he allied with Crimean Tatars to fight a "holy war" against the Poles in 1648: "Down with the Pany, the Jews and the Jesuits!"

FRANK L. FADNER, S.J.

Apparently there was even a Jesuit factor in the disability that almost hamstrung Peter the Great at the very beginning of his reign. The last act in the regency of his hated half-sister, the tsarevna Sof'ya Alekseevna, had been the Treaty of Nerchinsk, in which victorious Chinese interests had been represented by a Jesuit named Thomas Pereira. The regent herself had been somewhat sympathetic with the West and is said to have favored a union of the churches. She set up a Jesuit school in Moscow, which the Emperor Peter later brought to an end when, in 1719, he expelled the Fathers from his domains for the second time.

Such was the checkered pattern traced by the fortunes of the Society of Jesus in the Russias until the age of the Great Catherine II (1729–1796), her son, the Mad Tsar Paul, and her magnetic grandson, the first Alexander (1777–1825). For almost half a century, for a greater part of which most of the Christian world stood against the Jesuits, the court of Orthodox Imperial Russia extended special protection and patronage to them. It was during those years that a Russian motif was introduced into our own Georgetown story. And this is how this apparently strange anomaly of history came about.

It happens that in the year 1772 the tsaritsa Catherine II joined two other famous benevolent despots of Europe in carving up the historical place called Poland. As a result of this first operation, Polotsk, Vitebsk, Mogiliev, and White Russia became part of Catherine's empire. By the end of the century, after three such partitions of Poland, Minsk, all of Volhynia, Podolia, and Lithuania had suffered the same fate. This meant a formidable increase in the Roman Catholic population of the Russian Empire by about 1,600,000 souls.

Catherine the Great, whose one rule of thumb was the demand of expediency in her reliance on "circumstances, conjectures, and conjunctions," as she put it, was bound and determined not to increase her problems by needlessly tam-

Russia's Jesuit Province of COLLEGIUM GEORGEOPOLITANUM

pering with the institutions revered by her new subjects. Among these institutions were the schools and the missions of the Jesuits. These would have to be supported until perhaps one day her dream of a Catholic Church for Russified Poles, independent of Rome, might be realized! Almost immediately, in 1772, when some seventy-seven Jesuits of the Province of Mazovia became subjects of the Crown of Russia as a result of the first partition, the empress repealed Tsar Peter's ukase, which had intended to close Russia to the Jesuits forever.

It was on the 21st of July of the very next year, 1773, that the tragic Pope Clement XIV, harassed and fearful, yielded to the threats and demands that the Bourbon courts of Europe—Spain, France, Naples and Parma—had been making since 1768. Bent on the destruction of the Universal Church and the establishment of national state churches (as the Protestant historian Schoell points out), they demanded the universal suppression of the Jesuits. Louis XV and his agents, one of whom (Bernis) owed his Cardinal's hat to La Pompadour, had successfully exercised pressure for the election [as Pope Clement XIV] of a malleable Lorenzo Ganganelli, who feared the effect of a break with powerful secular governments on the peace of Christendom. With the preservation of that peace in his mind but with anguish in his soul, he signed and decreed (16 August) the famous bull *Dominus ac Redemptor*.[1] Jesuits in all parts of the world were put out of business by the Pontiff, who sadly remarked at the moment, *"Questa soppressione mi darà la morte!"*[2]

To be sure the great liquidation was to be effective in each country housing Jesuits only upon promulgation by the secular ruler of the place. The answer and the attitude of the Empress of all the Russias was a foregone conclusion. The Orthodox Empress of Russia refused to promulgate the brief of a Roman Pontiff, despite the request of the conscientious Jesuits themselves that she do so. Her partner in European real estate ventures, the Protestant Frederick II, disturbed by domestic problems similar to those of Russia, held out, too, for a while. After Frederick's death in 1786, however, the bull was promulgated in Prussia also. And so Jesuit colleges and missions continued to thrive in the Russian Empire in places like Polotsk,

FRANK L. FADNER, S.J.

Vitebsk, Orsha, Dünaburg (now Dougavpils, or Dvinsk, in Lithuania), and elsewhere.

The empress Catherine insisted on Jesuit freedom of action against the efforts of Archbishop Siestrzencewicz of Mogiliev to absorb them. She interceded with the new Pope, Pius VI, and the Russian Jesuits were allowed to open a novitiate, to conduct a congregation (the twentieth) in 1782 for the election of a vicar-general, Father Czerniewicz, and a vice-provincial, Father Kareu, and, in general, to carry on business as usual. For three months she and Potemkin discussed educational reforms for her empire with Father Czerniewiez at St. Petersburg. She encouraged Father Gruber, later General of the Society of Jesus, to open a training school for teachers, especially in the physical sciences. In May of 1780, the august empress with her friend Potemkin and other cronies visited the Jesuit establishment at Polotsk. There she attended Mass and heard an epic poem read in her honor by Very Reverend Father Rector, who echoed the sentiments of the Jesuit superior at Mogiliev in his explanation of the almost miraculous survival of the Jesuits in the Russian Empire: *"Clementissima imperatrice nostra protegente, populo derelicto exigente, Roma sciente et non contradicente."*[3]

It was Catherine who sent a special emissary to Rome, Canon Benislawski, a former Jesuit, to get formal papal approval of the existence of the Jesuits in Russia. The approval came at the end of a two-hour interview: *"Approbo Societatem Jesu in Alba Russia."*[4] This was later to be officially reaffirmed by the bull *Catholicae Fidei*[5] of 7 March 1801, just sixteen days before the assassination of Catherine's son, the so-called Mad Tsar Paul, who had asked Pope Pius VII for an official recognition of the Society. In general, the eccentric and cantankerous Emperor Paul so detested the memory of his notorious mother that he sought to reverse and undo everything she had accomplished during her long reign. The one exception was her policy of protecting the Jesuits. Paul multiplied the number of Jesuit colleges in Russia, enlarged the novitiate, installed Jesuits at the University of Vilna, and persuaded the Sultan to restore the Jesuit missions in the Aegean Archipelago!

Thus the first step toward the general restoration of the Je-

Russia's Jesuit Province of COLLEGIUM GEORGEOPOLITANUM

suits throughout the world, to be accomplished in 1814, was an imperial Russian manoeuvre.

In America, whither he had returned from Europe in 1774, John Carroll, future founder of Georgetown University and later archbishop of Baltimore, was overjoyed to learn of the circumstances surrounding the order of which he had been a member before its suppression. On September 26, 1783, upon learning that the Society of Jesus still existed in Russia, he wrote to his lifelong friend, Fr. Charles Plowden in Liege: "God grant that the little beginning in White Russia may have a foundation for erecting the Society once again; but I cannot help wishing that the protectress of it were a more respectable character than she has been represented." In the following year, at the suggestion of Benjamin Franklin, Father Carroll was recognized as superior of all Roman Catholics in the United States. In 1789 he became the country's first Catholic bishop and in 1808 was made archbishop at Baltimore.

It might be said, at least on the face of it, that the notorious Catherine entertained a somewhat more gracious and generous attitude toward the Jesuits than did this illustrious Catholic churchman toward her royal person. In a letter of 7 May 1779 she had assured her friend Baron Grimm, envoy of the Duke of Saxe-Gotha to France, that "neither I nor my honorable rogues, the Jesuits of White Russia, are going to cause the Pope any worry. They are very submissive to him and want to do only what he wishes. . . . You say that I am amusing myself by being kind to them. Assuredly you credit me with a pretty motive, whereas I have no other than that of keeping my word and seeking the public good. As for your grocers (the Bourbon kings), I make a present of them to you. . . ."

Later, on 12 September 1790, shocked by the bloody excesses of the French Revolution, the tsaritsa wrote again to Grimm:

> In bed I reflected over things, and, among others, I thought that one reason why the Mathieu de Montmorencys, the Noailes, and other prominent French families, etc., are

Frank L. Fadner, S.J.

so ill taught and so base in spirit that they are among the first promoters of the decree abolishing the nobility . . . is that the schools of the Jesuits have been abolished among you. Whatever you may say, those scamps looked well after the morals and tastes of the young people, and whatever is best in France came out of their schools.

On 12 March 1804 the Very Reverend Gabriel Gruber, brilliant fourth general of the Society of Jesus in Russia and once tutor of Catherine's son, the Tsarevich Paul, wrote from his residence in St. Petersburg to Bishop Carroll, explaining how, with papal approval, former Jesuits in America, as well as new aspirants, might be admitted into the Society surviving in Russia. Thus, through the affiliation of what they called "the Reverend Gentlemen formerly of the Society of Jesus in Maryland and Pennsylvania" with the Russian Society, the bishop was empowered in 1805 to reestablish the Jesuits in Maryland. North America's first Catholic bishop expressed the hope that ultimately the Society of Jesus would be restored throughout the world by the benevolent action of Orthodox Russia. And, he went on further to say to his friend, Father Plowden, "I should have most sanguine hopes of a union of the Greek and Latin churches." But more immediately the task of reviving Georgetown College, which he had founded in 1789, could now be seriously undertaken.

From 1782 to 1820, with papal approval and Imperial Russian patronage, scattered Jesuits throughout the world, through affiliation with the Russian Province, took orders from five generals resident in the Russian capital. These Jesuit generals were Stanyslaw Czerniewicz (successor to Lorenzo Ricci, who was general at the time of the suppression), 1782–83; Gabriel Lenkiewicz, 1785–98; Francis Kareu, 1799–1802; Gabriel Gruber, 1802–5; and Thadeusz Brzozowski, 1805–20. By the end of a period partially coinciding with the reign of three Russian rulers, there were Jesuit missions all along the Volga and, from 1810, in faraway Astrakhan and the Caucasus.

By the time Father General Brzozowski died in St. Peters-

Russia's Jesuit Province of COLLEGIUM GEORGEOPOLITANUM

burg in 1820, the Society of Jesus had been restored by Pius VII, in 1814, and because of the universal scope now envisaged for its activities, provision was made for the election of a new general, Aloysius Fortis. It was determined that the Superior of the restored Society was to reside in Rome, as had been the practice before the suppression.

This the megalomaniac Tsar Alexander unfortunately could not tolerate. Hence in 1820, with the death of Russia's last Jesuit general, Father Brzozowski (whom the jealous emperor in 1814 had actually refused to allow to go to Rome to receive the bull of restoration from the hands of the Pope), the Russian theme in Jesuit history came to an end. The Society was formally expelled, with little rancor and no violence, from the Russian empire that had harbored it for almost fifty years.

Without a doubt, whatever the motivations were, the rulers of Russia had conferred a great boon, materially, on the numerous centers of learning now restored to the Society throughout the world. Those places could make good use of the 358 men of all nationalities and varieties of talent resident in Russia at the time of their expulsion from the empire.

In 1819, just before his death and the expulsion of his Society from Russia, Father General Brzozowski drew up a catalogue of the Russian province and transmitted it to Rome. In it the reader will find listed as part of that Russian province *"Collegium Georgiopolitanum penes Urbem Washington in Marylandia,"*[6] with four priests, twenty scholastics, and a dozen coadjutor brothers living and working at the place. Of the Jesuit Fathers who lived in Russia during the age of the Suppression, at least half a dozen died in Maryland.

All of this is indicative of the historical fact that early affairs at Georgetown University were for a considerable period directed from Russian headquarters. Father General Gruber in 1805 authorized Bishop Carroll to appoint the Jesuit Father Robert Molyneux as superior of the American Jesuits affiliated with the Society in Russia. Father Molyneux had been Georgetown's (second) president, from 1793 to 1796, and was

Frank L. Fadner, S.J.

so again from 1806 to 1808. It was Father General Brzozowski who appointed the fabulous Father John Anthony Grassi as the seventh president of Georgetown (1812–1817) and successfully insisted that the Society of Jesus should have full control of the college founded by John Carroll.

The Italian-born Father Grassi came to Georgetown from Russia, where he had received all his Jesuit training and where he was ordained a priest. Before his assignment to America this brilliant man had been rector of the Jesuit college in Polotsk and the College of Nobles at St. Petersburg. He had been designated to head an abortive mission to China by an admiring Russian government.

It was the same Jesuit superior in Russia who sent Father Francis Malevé to Georgetown in 1806, as well as Father Peter Epinette, who taught philosophy here. Others like Adam Britt, John Henry, and a Father Brown, were assigned to labor in the neighboring territory of Maryland. In 1842, Father Fidelis de Grivel died at Georgetown. He had entered the Society in distant Polotsk and, thirty years later, was master of novices at Georgetown when Maryland was set up as a province. Again it was from Russia that Georgetown was to draw its ninth president. This was the illustrious Reverend Anthony Kohlmann, who became a Jesuit at Dünaburg in the Russian Empire. He arrived here from Russia in 1806, when Georgetown accommodated less than thirty students. He was to become master of novices at Georgetown, superior of the entire mission, and finally president of Georgetown in 1818.

All in all, it must be admitted that increased manpower from Russia, the only center of Jesuit survival between 1773 and 1814, played a significant role in the survival of Georgetown College, which in those precarious times might easily have expired. Through the meandering course of history, with its strange interplay of circumstances and human motivations of varying quality, it came to pass that the lands of Russia should see the preservation of the link between what Jesuits like to call the old Society and the new. *Collegium Georgiopolitanum*, an early experiment in American liberal education, was a symbol of that connection.

Russia's Jesuit Province of COLLEGIUM GEORGEOPOLITANUM

ENDNOTES

1 "Lord and Redeemer"
2 "This suppression will be the death of me!"
3 "With our most clement empress protecting, with the neglected people demanding, with Rome knowing and not contradicting."
4 "I approve the Society of Jesus in White Russia"
5 "Of the Catholic Faith"
6 "Georgetown College within the City of Washington in Maryland"

CHAPTER 3

The State of Individuals 1776–1976

CARROLL QUIGLEY

In his basic course on World Civilizations, Carroll Quigley captivated many students by the breadth of his sometimes unconventional ideas and the power of his discourse. Notable among his major works as a comparative civilizationist and analyst of world historical systems was *Tragedy and Hope: A History of the World in Our Time* (Macmillan, 1966). In October 1976, when he had recently retired after forty years of teaching, Professor Quigley delivered the first Oscar Iden Lecture Series to an audience composed chiefly of his colleagues and former students. In three lectures, he tackled one of his long-standing intellectual concerns, the growth of authority and the state over the previous thousand years of Western history. The first lectures covered "The State of Communities, 976–1576" and "The State of Estates, 1576–1776." Herewith the third.

SOURCE: Carroll Quigley (with editorial assistance by Helen Veit), *Public Authority and the State in the Western Tradition: A Thousand Years of Growth, 976–1976*, The Oscar Iden Lectures (School of Foreign Service, Georgetown University, 1977), pp. 26–40.

The State of Individuals 1776–1976

To Satisfy Human Needs

This is the most difficult of the lectures on the history of the thousand years of the growth of public authority. What happened in the last two hundred years is fairly clear to me, but it is not easy to convey, even to those of you who are familiar with the framework of much of my thinking. One reason for this difficulty, clearly, is the complexity of the subject itself; but then the preceding eight hundred years were quite as complex as the last two hundred. A much more fundamental reason for the difficulty is this: The reality of the last two hundred years of the history of Western civilization, including the history of our own country, is not reflected in the general brainwashing you have received, in the political mythology you have been hearing, or in the historiography of the period as it exists today.

I will divide the period from 1776 to 1976 into two parts. The first, to about 1890, was a period of expansion of industrial society; the last approximately eighty years have been an age of profound crisis, not only in our own country, but in Western civilization—the unit in which I carry on my thinking on the subject. To deal with this period, I have to go back to fundamentals, and particularly to the fundamentals of human values, and to do that, we must have paradigms.

The whole thousand years, as I explained in my first lecture, is a shift from a society in 976 made up of communities to a society today composed both of states of monstrous power and of atomized individuals. I will use certain definitions: *A society is an organization of persons and artifacts*—things made by people—to satisfy human needs. It would not exist if it had not come into existence to satisfy human needs. Notice: I do not say human desires. One of the striking things about our society today is the remoteness of our desires from our needs. If you ask anyone what he wants, what he desires, he will give you lists of things as remote as can be from human needs.

In our society, the process we have been tracing for a thousand years is the growth of the state. As I indicated in the first lecture, a state is not the same thing as a society, although the Greeks and Romans thought it was. *A state* is an organization of power on a territorial basis. The link between a society, whether it is made up of communities or individuals, and a state is this: *Power rests on the ability to satisfy human needs.*

The "Levels of Culture." Now I will put on the board something with which former students are familiar—the levels of culture, the aspects of a society: military, political, economic, social, emotional, religious, intellectual. Those are your basic human needs, arranged in an evolutionary sequence. Millions of years ago, even before our species became humans, we had a need for defense of the group, because it is perfectly obvious that our species cannot live outside of groups. We can satisfy our needs only by cooperating within a group. Indeed, humans will not become human unless they grow up in communities. We will come back to that because it is the basis of this lecture.

If you have a group, it must be defended against outsiders; that is *military*. Even before men came out of the trees they had that need. If your needs are to be satisfied within some kind of a group, you must have ways of settling disputes and arguments and reconciling individual problems within the group; that is *political*. You must have organizational patterns for satisfying material needs, food, clothing, and shelter; that is *economic*.

Then came two needs that have been largely destroyed or frustrated in the last thousand years of Western civilization. People have *social* needs. They have a need for other people; they have a need to love and to be loved. They have a need to be noticed. Sirhan Sirhan killed Robert Kennedy because no one had ever noticed him and he was determined that, from then on, someone would know he existed. In fact, most of these

The State of Individuals 1776–1976

"motiveless" assassinations are of this type. Someone went up to the top of the University of Texas tower and shot something like seventeen people before they caught him. That was because no one had ever noticed him. People need other people. That is the social need. The basis of social interrelationships is reciprocity: if you cooperate with others, others will cooperate with you.

The next is the *emotional* need. Humans must have emotional experiences. This is obtained in two ways that I can see: moment-to-moment relationships with other people and moment-to-moment relationships with nature. Our society has so cluttered up our lives with artifacts—television sets or automobiles or whatever—and organizational structures that moment-to-moment relationships with nature are almost impossible. Most people do not even know what the weather outside is like. Someone said recently that we had just had a great drought here in Washington, and four or five people standing there said, "That's ridiculous." We had a shortage of about eight inches of rain, I believe, but no one noticed it. Because they are in buildings, it does not matter to them whether it is raining or not.

The next need is the *religious*. It became fashionable in Western civilization, particularly in the last hundred years, to be scornful of religion. But it is a fact that human beings have religious needs. They have a need for a feeling of certitude in their minds about things they cannot control and do not fully understand and, with humility, will admit they do not understand. When you destroy people's religious expressions, they will establish secularized religions like Marxism.

People also have *intellectual* needs. I used to tell students that Marilyn Monroe had profound intellectual needs. And when no one would treat her as an intellect or even as a potential intellect, she became starved for intellectual experience. That's why she married a man like Arthur Miller: she thought he was an intellectual.

So, those are human needs. Power is the ability to satisfy those needs. And someone who says that power is organized force, or that power is the outcome of an election, or that power is the ability to cut off our supply of oil, has a completely inadequate way of looking at it. My experience and study of the destruction of civilizations and the collapse of great empires have convinced me that empires and civilizations do not collapse because of deficiencies on the military or political level. The Roman army never met an army that was better than it was. But the Roman army could not be sustained when everything had collapsed and no one cared. No one wanted to serve, no one wanted to pay taxes, no one cared.

Individuals, Communities, and States. Now you must put these things together to some extent. Persons, or personalities if you wish, can be made only in communities. A *community* is made up of intimate relationships among diverse types of individuals—a kinship group, or a local group, a neighborhood, a village, a large family. Without communities, no infant will be sufficiently socialized. A boy may grow up to be forty years old, he may have made an extremely good living, he may have engendered half a dozen children, but he is still an infant unless he has been properly socialized, and that occurs in the first four or five years of life.

In our society today, we have attempted to throw the whole burden of socializing our population upon the school system, to which the individual arrives only at the age of four or five. A few years ago there were big programs to take children to school for a few hours at age two and three and four, but such programs will not socialize them. The first two years are important. The way a child is treated in the first two *days* is of vital importance. He has to be loved; above all, he has to be talked to.

A state of individuals, such as we have now reached in Western civilization, will not create persons. The atomized individuals who make it up will be motivated by desires that do not necessarily reflect needs. Instead of needing other people, they need a shot of heroin; instead of some kind of religious conviction, they have to be with the winning team.

Human needs are the basis of power. The state, as I said, is a power structure on a territorial basis, and the state will sur-

The State of Individuals 1776–1976

vive only if it has sufficient ability to satisfy enough of these needs. It is not enough for it to have organized force, and when a politician says "Elect me President and I will establish law and order," he means organized force or organized power of other kinds. On this complex point I will simply say here that the object of the political level is to legitimize power: that is, to get people, in their minds, to recognize and accept the actual power relationship in their society.

Next Tuesday a decision will be made as to who will be President of the United States. That will not necessarily reflect the actual power relationships in the United States at all. If all the people who are intellectually frustrated would vote, the result might be quite different. Many of you have come to these lectures because you are intellectually frustrated, and you want to be exposed again to my insistent demands that you think about things.

We no longer have intellectually satisfying arrangements in our educational system, in our arts, humanities, or anything else; instead we have slogans and ideologies. An ideology is a religious or emotional expression; it is not an intellectual expression. So in the last couple of centuries when a society is reaching its end, you have what I call misplacement of satisfactions. You find your emotional satisfaction in making a lot of money, or in being elected to the White House in 1972, or in proving to the poor, half-naked people of Southeast Asia that you can kill them in large numbers.

The Sovereign State. The state is a good state if it is sovereign and if it is responsible. It is more or less incidental whether a state is, for example, democratic. If democracy reflects the structure of power in the society, then the state should be democratic. But if the pattern of power in a society is not democratic, then you cannot have a democratic state. This is what has happened in some countries in Latin America, Africa, and similar places: when they have an election and the army does not like the man who is elected, they move in and throw him out. The outcome of the election does not reflect the power situation, in which organized force is the dominant thing.

Carroll Quigley

When I say governments have to be responsible, I am saying the same thing as when I said they have to be legitimate: they must reflect the power structure of the society. Politics is the area for establishing responsibility by legitimizing power, that is, by somehow demonstrating the power structure to people; and it may take a revolution, such as the French Revolution, and it may take a war, like the American Civil War. In the American Civil War, for example, the structure of power in the United States was such—perhaps unfortunately, I don't know—that the South could not leave unless the North was willing. It was that simple. But it took a war to prove it.

Sovereignty has eight aspects: (1) defense; (2) judicial—settling disputes; (3) administrative—discretionary actions for the public need; (4) taxation—mobilizing resources (this is one of the powers the French government did not have in 1776); (5) legislation—the finding of rules and establishment of rules through promulgation and statute; (6) executive—the enforcement of laws and judicial decisions. Then there are two which are of absolutely paramount importance today: (7) monetary—the creation and control of money and credit—if that is not an aspect of the public sovereignty, then the state is far less than fully sovereign; and (8) the incorporating power—the right to say that an association of people is a fictitious person with the right to hold property and to sue and be sued in the courts. Notice: the federal government of the United States today does not have the seventh and eighth, but I'll come back to that later.

Then and Now. If we go back before 976, when there were communities, the main core of people's lives and experience that controlled their behavior and determined their desires—controls and rewards, I call it—was in the religious, emotional, and social levels. They had religious beliefs, and they had social and emotional relationships with the people they saw every day. That was the core of their lives. The significant thing is that those controls and rewards were internalized, acquired very largely in the first four or five years of life. When a child is born, he or she is not a person, but only a human being. A child

The State of Individuals 1776–1976

is utterly potential. When persons become personalities, such as we ourselves, then they have traits that they acquired out of their potentialities as the result of experiences over numerous years.

This is why people could get along without a state in 976: all the significant controls were internalized. I took the year 976 because, although Western civilization had come into existence about two hundred years before that, in 976 it began to expand, producing more goods per person per day or per year. You know what I mean by expansion if you took my freshman course: increased output per capita, increased knowledge, increased geographic area for the civilization itself, and increased population. That began in 976.

The economic expansion was achieved chiefly by specialization and exchange: instead of each little group's trying to satisfy all its own needs, groups began to concentrate, for example to produce only wool and exchange it for other things. That process of increasing specialization and exchange, which is the basis of expansion in our civilization, I call *commercialization*. As long as the society is expanding, that process of commercialization will continue, as it has for a thousand years in our society, where today everything is commercialized, politics, religion, education, ideology, belief, the armed services. Practically everything is commercialized; everything has its price.

When this expansion reaches a crisis, you get increasing *politicization:* The expansion is slowing up, and you are no longer attempting to achieve increased output per capita, or increased wealth, or increased satisfactions, or whatever is motivating you, by economic expansion, but are going to do it by mobilizing power. We have seen this going on in our society for almost a century.

And then, as the society continues and does not reform, you get increased *militarization*. You can certainly see that process in Western civilization and in the history of the United States. In the last forty years our society has been drastically militarized. It is not yet as militarized as other societies and other periods have been; we still have a long way to go in this direction—a couple of centuries to go, I would guess, although things are moving faster than they did in any civilization before this one.

As this process goes on, you get certain other things. I've hinted at a number of them. One is misplacement of satisfactions. You find your satisfactions—your emotional satisfaction, your social satisfaction—not in moment-to-moment relationships with nature and with other people, but with power, or with wealth, or even with organized force—sadism, in some cases: Go out and murder a lot of people in a war, a just war, naturally.

The second thing that occurs as this goes on is an increasing remoteness of desires from needs, followed by an increasing confusion between means and ends. The ends are human needs; but if I asked people what these needs are, they could hardly tell me. Instead they would want the means they have been brainwashed to accept, that they think will satisfy their needs. But it is perfectly obvious that the methods we have been using are not working. Never was any society in human history as rich and as powerful as Western civilization and the United States, and it is not a happy society. Just this week, I looked at a book called *The Joyless Economy* by economist Tibor Scitovsky, who diagrammed some of these things.

In the final aspect of this process, controls on behavior shift from the intermediate levels of human experience—social, emotional, and religious—to the lower—military and political—or to the upper—ideological. They become the externalized controls of a mature civilization: weapons, police, bureaucracies, material rewards, or ideology. Customary conformity is replaced by conscious decision-making, and this usually implies a shift from your own conformity to someone else's decision. In its final stages, the civilization becomes a dualism of almost totalitarian imperial power and an amorphous mass culture of atomized individuals.

All of that is for the sake of establishing a few paradigms.

The State of Individuals 1776–1976

WHAT HAPPENED AFTER 1776?

In 1776, Western civilization was approaching a revolutionary situation. A revolutionary situation is one in which the structure of power—real power—is not reflected in the structure of law, institutions, and conventional arrangements. Law and legal arrangements, including constitutional structures, were not legitimate in much of Western civilization in 1776. They were not responsible because they did not reflect power. Whether it was the English Parliament, which had a legal right to rule America; or the nightmarish constitution of France, which no longer reflected the structure of power in French society in any way; or, east of the Rhine, the enlightened despotisms—the laws of the polity did not reflect the power structure of Europe at all, as Napoleon very soon showed them. This, therefore, was a revolutionary situation.

Let us look a little more closely at these.

In England, the laws of the polity established control of the country in an oligarchy of landowners, the Whig oligarchy. Members of the House of Commons were sent to Parliament by pieces of land, and anyone who owned a piece of land with the right to send a member to Parliament could do so whether anyone lived on the piece of land or not. It was not a reflection of the power structure of England to say that pieces of land were powerful. I do not have to demonstrate to you that the legal arrangements by which the British Parliament made rules to govern life in the United States were equally unrealistic.

In Central Europe we had what was called enlightened despotism: small principalities ruled by despots who had a legal right to say, "This will happen; that will happen; something else will happen." In the period from 1776 onward, for about twenty-five years, they tried to establish a more rational life in their principalities, but they couldn't do it. Their systems of weights and measures—I won't attempt to describe them to you—were absolute, unholy chaos. They had a different weight or measurement for every city and those measurements changed as you went from village to village or from district to district. They also had been changing in size for hundreds of years, because the power of the creditors was so great: if you

Carroll Quigley

owed a bushel of wheat to your landlord, all the landlords together, over generations, could make the bushel a larger measure.

In Eastern Europe in this period Poland disappeared, because the Polish landlord class preferred to keep their serfs than be politically independent. They were unwilling to organize a modern army with modern weapons and modern military training to defend Poland against outside enemies, such as Prussia, Russia, or Austria. As a result, those three got together and divided up Poland in 1795, so Poland no longer existed. Under Napoleon there was a Grand Duchy of Warsaw, but Poland did not exist again until 1919.

In France the polity had reached a condition of total paralysis. The government did not have sovereignty. It did not have the taxing power; it did not have the legislative power; it did not have the incorporating power; it did not have the judicial power; it did not have most of the eight aspects of sovereignty. And in 1776 the government became aware of this when they tried to abolish the guilds and could not do so, because under the law the guilds could not be abolished unless their debts were paid. The government could not pay their debts because it did not have the taxing power. And it did not have the taxing power because it did not have the judicial power: if it took someone to court, the judges would say, "No, you have no right to examine his income. You can ask him only what he has been paying for the last couple of hundred years on that piece of property (or whatever it is)."

The result was the explosion of the French Revolution, which produced, by the time of Napoleon, let us say 1805, the most sovereign state in Europe. Notice: Napoleon was an enlightened despot, the last one in Europe. Anyone who says, as does Robert Palmer, for one, that France was leading the parade in 1789 in terms of government and public authority, just does not know what he is talking about. In 1789 France was bringing up the absolute rear as far as public authority and sovereignty were concerned. That is why France got its enlightened despot so late. He was not even a Frenchman; he was an Italian—and he imposed an Italian government on France. Because it was so

The State of Individuals 1776–1976

rational, so powerful, so well-organized, and the new sovereignty was embodied in a new entity, the nation, it had a power that made it possible for Napoleon to conquer almost all of Europe. He was ultimately defeated, though, as most conquerors of all Europe have been throughout history, witness Henry V of England in the early fifteenth century, Philip II in the sixteenth century, Wilhelm II in 1918, and Hitler in 1945.

After Napoleon: The Long-running Age of Expansion. By 1820, after the Napoleonic system had been replaced, however unstable these four geographical zones I have mentioned may have been, they were much more stable, and much more legitimate, than they had been in 1776. And although in 1820 they were fundamentally not that stable, we know there was political stability in Europe for at least three generations after that date, until at least the 1860s (we won't go into the brief war in 1866). That stability of Europe from 1815 to about 1885 is something on which we now look with nostalgia.

The reasons for this apparent stability had nothing to do with the structure of the state, except for the degree to which it had become rationalized and sovereign through the period of revolution from 1776 to about 1820. With additional events, the situation looked like stability, and these additional events produced a new Age of Expansion.

The first of these events was the *expansion of technology,* including the Agricultural and Industrial Revolutions. The Agricultural Revolution of about 1720 and onward made it possible to produce more and more food from land with less and less labor. The Industrial Revolution began about 1750 and was the application of inanimate energy to the production process on a large scale. (Incidentally, 1776 is a very significant year, and this is not just because the American Revolution began during it. Among other occurrences, Watt's patent of the steam engine was in 1776; Adam Smith's *Wealth of Nations* was published in 1776; and the failure of the French to reorganize their political system occurred in 1776.) The disruption of communities, the destruction of religion, and the frustration of emotions were greatly intensified by the Industrial Revolution: by its railroads and factories, the growth of cities, and the technological revolution in the countryside and in the growing of food.

The appearance of stability in the nineteenth century Age of Expansion was also due to the *externalization of rewards and controls*. This eventually brought on an acceleration of the main focus of society's activities downward again in the levels of culture, from the areas of internal controls to the areas of external controls. If you can be bought, with a higher salary, to go to San Diego and give up all your friends and associations, that is an external control. If you can be forced to go there by power, if you can be sent there by the draft, that is militarization.

Modern Myths. Another thing which became very obvious in the nineteenth century was the *increasing role of propaganda* for the purpose of changing people's ways of looking at society. The success of this propaganda helped to create an impression of stability. At the beginning of the lecture, I offended some of you by saying you have been brainwashed. That is not an insult; it is a simple statement of fact. When an infant is born and socialized in a society, even if he is socialized to become a mature individual, he has been brainwashed. That is, he has been given a structure for categorizing his experience and a system of values applied to that structuring or categories.

But in our society, in the nineteenth and twentieth centuries, this socializing process has become a propagandist system in which increasing emphasis is put on the future: Think only of the future. This is the ideology against which the young people of the 1960s and 1970s rebelled. Future preference: plan; study hard; save. All the things I used to hear from my maiden aunts: "Wise bees save honey; wise boys save money," and they each secretly gave me a dollar as I was leaving. "A penny saved is a penny earned." "A stitch in time..."—everything that's in *Poor Richard*, the Benjamin Franklin propaganda machine.

Another aspect of this nineteenth century propaganda system is the *increasing emphasis upon material desires*. If you had the material things you wanted—a nice house in the suburbs, a swimming pool, a couple of big cars, a place in the country, a motor boat, a trailer to take it back and forth—you should be

The State of Individuals 1776–1976

happy and satisfied. Now the list is endless—a pocket computer, citizens' band radio, whatever you want.

A third idea we were brainwashed into believing was that the only important thing was *individualism*. They called it freedom. There is no such thing as freedom. There is something called liberty; it is quite different. Freedom is freedom from restraints. We are always under restraints. The difference between a stable society and an unstable one is that the restraints in an unstable one are external. In a stable society, government ultimately becomes unnecessary; people are self-disciplined, and the restraints on people's actions are internal. They are the restraints you have accepted because they make it possible for you to satisfy all your needs and desires to the degree that is good for you.

Another thing they have brainwashed us into believing in the last 150 years is that *quantitative change* is superior to any qualitative attributes. In other words, if we can turn out more automobiles this year than last, it doesn't matter if they're half as good. The same is true of everything. We are quantifying everything, and this is why we are now trying to put everything on computers. Governments no longer have to make decisions; the computers will do it.

Another thing they have succeeded in doing is to give us *vicarious satisfactions* for many of our frustrations. It is unbelievable to see how the American people are hung up on vicarious experiences: television, movies, mass spectator sports. You have no idea what the small towns and cities of America are like on Friday nights, when the local high school football or basketball team is engaged in competition with their neighbor eighteen miles away. And what a gloomy place the chapel or church is Sunday morning if they lose. People need exercise; they do not need to watch other people exercise, particularly people who have already had too much exercise. Another vicarious satisfaction is the sexy magazine; this is vicarious sex. To anyone rushing out to buy one, I'd like to say, "The real thing is better."

The brainwashing which has been going on for 150 years has also resulted in the replacement of intellectual activities and religion by *ideologies and science*. It is hardly possible today to discuss the problems of the historical past without running up against Marxist interpretations. I have nothing against Marx, except that his theories do not explain what happened, and this, to me, is a fatal defect. The very idea that there is some kind of conflict between science and religion is completely mistaken. Science is a method for investigating experience, and religion is something quite different. Religion is the fundamental, necessary internalization of your system of more permanent values.

Another thing they have tried to get us to believe in the last 150 years—and the idea is now dying in front of us—is the myth that *the nation as the repository of sovereignty* can be both a state and a community. This is the great ideological innovation of the French Revolution, you see. The nation can be the repository of sovereignty. But suppose weapons systems in a society are such that it is possible for a government to impose its will over an area a thousand miles across. And suppose that in that thousand mile area there are a number of nations, such as the Bretons, the Catalonians, the Welsh, the Lithuanians. These are as much nations as the ones that somehow or other became the embodiments of sovereignty in the nineteenth century.

Why did the English, the French, the Castilians, the Hohenzollerns, and others become the repositories of sovereignty as nations? They did so because, at that time, weapons systems made it possible to compel obedience over areas approximately the same size as those inhabited by the national groups I have mentioned. As a result, those with the weapons were able to crush other nationalisms, such as the Scots, the Welsh, the Irish, the Catalonians (who had a much longer and more cultured history than the Castilians), the Provençals, and many others.

In other words, nationalism is an episode in history, and it fit a certain power structure and a certain configuration of human life in our civilization. Now what's happening? They all want autonomy. The Scots think they can get their independence and control the oil in the North Sea, and then England will become a colonial area for Edinburgh.

The State of Individuals 1776–1976

The True State of the State. In 1820, the state was thus essentially unstable, in spite of appearances. It was not fully sovereign. It did not, for example, have the control of money and credit in most places; it did not have control of corporations in most places. It was not stable because the nation is not a satisfactory community. The very idea that, because everyone who speaks French is in the same nation and, in the nineteenth century, in the same state, they must therefore be in the same community, is just not true. The nation or the state, as we now have it in terms of the structure of power, cannot be a community.

Another thing that may serve to point out the instability of the power system of the state: the individual cannot be made the basic unit of society, as we have tried to do, or of the state, since the internalization of controls must be the preponderant influence in any stable society. Even in a society in which it appears that all power is in the hands of the government—Soviet Russia, let's say—at least 80 percent of all human behavior is regulated by internalized controls socialized in the people by the way they were treated from the moment they were born. As a result, they have come to accept certain things that allow the Soviet state to act as if it can do anything, when it obviously cannot and knows it cannot.

Weapons Again. Also related to the problem of internalized controls is the shift of weapons in our society. This is a profound problem, and I have spent ten years studying it throughout all of history. The shift of weapons in any civilization and, above all, in our civilization, from shock weapons to missile weapons has a dominant influence on the ability to control individuals: Individuals cannot be controlled by missile weapons.

If you go back several hundred years to the Middle Ages, all weapons were shock weapons, that is, you came at the enemy with a spear or a sword. Even as late as 1916, in the First World War, you came at the enemy with bayonets after a preliminary barrage with artillery. But we have now shifted almost completely to missile weapons. Missile weapons are weapons that you hurl. You may shoot, you may drop bombs from an airplane, you may throw a hand grenade: these are missile weapons.

Carroll Quigley

The essential difference between a shock weapon and a missile weapon is this: a missile weapon is either fired or it isn't fired. It cannot be half-fired. Once you let it go, it is out of your control. It is a killing weapon. But a shock weapon—a billy club or a bayonet—can be used to any degree you wish. If you say to someone, "Get out of the room," and you pull out a machine gun, or you call in a B-52 bomber, or you pull the pin in a hand grenade . . . ? But with a bayonet, you can persuade him.

In our society, individual behavior can no longer be controlled by any system of weaponry we have. In fact, we do not have enough people, even if we equip them with shock weapons, to control the behavior of that part of the population which does not have internalized controls. One reason for that is clearly that the 20 percent who do not have internalized controls are concentrated in certain areas. Nor can guerrilla resistance, terrorism, and the rest be controlled by any system or organized structure of force that exists, at least on a basis of missile weaponry (and, as I said, shock weaponry would take too many people).

We have now done what the Romans did when they started to commit suicide: We have shifted from an army of citizen soldiers to an army of mercenaries, and those mercenaries are being recruited in our society, as they were in Roman society, from the 20 percent of the population that lacks the internalized controls of the civilization.

The Misguided Nineteenth Century. The appearance of stability from 1840 to about 1900 was superficial, temporary, and destructive in the long run, because, as I've said, you must have communities, and communities and societies must rest upon cooperation and not on competition. Anyone who says that society can be run on the basis of everyone's trying to maximize his own greed is talking total nonsense. All the history of human society shows that it is nonsense. And to teach it in the schools, and to go on television and call it the American way of life, does not make it true. *Competition and envy cannot become the basis of any society or any community.*

The economic and technological achievements of industri-

The State of Individuals 1776–1976

alization in this period were also fundamentally mistaken. (I'll try not to get too technical.) The economic expansion of industrialization has been based on plundering the natural capital of the globe that was created over millions of years: plundering the soils of their fertility; plundering human communities, whether our own or someone else's, in Africa or anywhere else; or plundering the forest. In 1776 the wealth of forest in North America was beyond belief; within 150 years, it had been destroyed and more than 90 percent of it wasted. And it had in it three hundred years of accumulated capital savings and investment of sunlight and soil fertility. (And now that our bread is going to have five times as much fiber by being made out of sawdust, we are going to have to go on plundering the forests to an even larger degree; this, I am sure, is one of the reasons why two days ago President Ford signed the new bill allowing clear-cutting in the National Forests. We need that roughage or fiber in our bread—having taken all the natural fiber out of the wheat and thrown it away.)

The energy that gave us the Industrial Revolution—coal, oil, natural gas—represented the accumulated sunlight that managed somehow to be saved in the earth out of three billion years of sunshine. That is what the fossil fuels are. This is not income to be spent; this is capital to be saved and invested. But we have wasted it.

WHAT IS WRONG WITH TWENTIETH CENTURY SOCIETY

The fundamental, all-pervasive cause of world instability today is the destruction of communities by the commercialization of all human relationships and the resulting neuroses and psychoses. The technological acceleration of transportation, communications, and weapons systems is now creating power areas wider than existing political structures. We still have at least half a dozen political structures in Europe in the 1970s, but our technology and the power system of Western civilization today are such that most of Europe should be a single power system. This creates instability.

Medical science and the population explosion have continued

to produce more and more people when the supply of food and the supply of jobs are becoming increasingly precarious, not only in the United States, but everywhere, because the whole purpose of using fossil fuels in the corporate structure is to eliminate jobs. "Labor-saving," we call it, as if there were something wrong with working. Working is one of the joys of life. And if we have created a society in which working is a pain in the neck, then we have created a society not fit for human beings. (It will be obvious to you that I have enjoyed my work, although now, at the end of my career, I have no conviction that I did any good. Fortunately, I had a marvelous father and a marvelous mother, who taught us that you do not have to win, you just have to give it all you've got.)

To get back to sovereignty and the structure of the state, another cause of today's instability is that we now have a society in America, Europe, and much of the world that is totally dominated by the two elements of sovereignty that are *not* included in the state structure: control of credit and banking and the corporation. These are free of political controls and social responsibility, and they have largely monopolized power in Western civilization and in American society. They are ruthlessly going forward to eliminate land, labor, entrepreneurial-managerial skills, and everything else the economists once told us were the chief elements of production. The only element of production they are concerned with is the one they can control: capital.

So now everything is capital-intensive, including medicine, and it has not worked. I'll give you just one example. No one has a more capital intensive medical system than the United States, and many of you may be well satisfied with it. I simply want to point out a couple of facts. Let us look at a ten-year-old boy in the United States today. His expectation of life is less than that in thirty other countries, according to United Nations statistics. We pay more than the people in any of those thirty countries for a capital-intensive medical system devoted to keeping people who are almost dead alive a few more days, instead of making people grow up healthy by teaching them that work is fun, that they don't have to be gluttons—in the

The State of Individuals 1776–1976

United States, more than half of our food is wasted, maybe because it is not that good. Exercise, moderation, and the like—it is all the old stuff we used to get in Sunday School. It just happens to be correct.

Our agricultural system is another cause of instability. It used to be a system in which seed was put into the earth to create food by taking sunlight, rain, and the wealth of the soil, but we have replaced it with an agricultural system that is entirely capital-intensive. We have eliminated labor and have even eliminated land to a considerable extent, so that we now pour out what we call food, but what is really a chemical synthetic. We have done this by putting a larger and larger amount of chemical fertilizers and pesticides from fossil fuels into a smaller and smaller amount of soil. To give you one figure: Every bushel of corn we send to the Russians represents one gallon of gasoline. And then they tell us that by selling our grain to the Russians we are earning the foreign exchange that will allow us to pay for petroleum at fourteen dollars a barrel. No one has stopped to ask how many gallons were used to grow that grain and send it to the Russians.

In the thirty years from 1940 to 1970, three million American farms were abandoned because the families who worked them could not compete with the corporate farmers using the new chemical methods of producing crops. Thirty million people left these abandoned farms and rural areas and went into the towns and cities, millions of them to get on relief. In 1970, two thousand farms a year were going out of production. These are the farms on which we brought up your grandparents, the people who won the Civil War, indeed, the people who fought in the First World War and, in many cases, even in the Second. Will the tractors be able to fight the next war when there are no more farm boys to fight? (Of course, whether there are farm boys or not, they won't want to fight.)

In a similar way, by urban renewal and other things, we are destroying communities in the cities. Much of the legislation of the last forty years in this country has been aimed at the destruction of families, neighborhoods, ghettos, parishes, and any other communities.

Carroll Quigley

All these processes create frustrations on every level of human experience, and result in the instability and disorder we see around us every day.

The Crisis in America's Governance

Now I come to a topic of some delicacy: the United States constitutional crisis. The three branches of government set up in 1789 do not contain the eight aspects of sovereignty. The Constitution completely ignores, for example, the administrative power. The result is that the three branches of government have been struggling ever since to decide which of them will control the administrative power. The growth of political parties was necessary to establish relationships among the three branches. And as a result of the way the three branches were set up, each has tried to go outside the very sphere in which it should be restrained.

Another aspect of our constitutional crisis can be summed up in what young Schlesinger—that's Arthur Schlesinger, Jr.—called the Imperial Presidency. When I look at the president of the United States, what I see is Caesar Augustus. He is commander-in-chief; that's what *imperator*, emperor, means. He is the head of the executive branch. He is the head of state, which means he is the representative of the United States government in all foreign affairs and all ambassadors are accredited to him. He is the head of his political party. And, he is head of the administrative system, which is increasingly making all the decisions as to what will be spent and who will spend it. Do you know who is making the decisions in our Bureau of Management and Budget as to who will get how much?

The president is also the symbol of national unity, the focus of our emotional feelings regarding our country. This is one of the reasons why it is so difficult to get rid of an incumbent president, either by election or by impeachment.

We have today a general paralysis of government in the United States, especially in the administrative power, by the very thing we praise most: the so-called rule of law, which should rather be called the rule of lawyers. Let me give you one example. It is perfectly clear in the Constitution that a president

The State of Individuals 1776–1976

can be impeached by a vote of the Congress: indictment by the House, conviction by the Senate. This does not require common law procedures; it does not require judicial process. It is not a judicial action at all. It is a simple political action: if you have the votes, he can be removed, simply by counting them.

The horrible thing about the whole Nixon business is that impeachment will never again be used in the history of the United States, because every member of the Judiciary Committee has to be a lawyer, and the Judiciary Committee has to recommend impeachment. And they require all kinds of procedures you would use in a court of law if you were accused of holding up a bank. The result is that never again will anyone try to impeach a president. It would take years and be indecisive, when you could simply have taken a vote and had the whole thing done in one morning.

There are a lot of other things in the Constitution that are perfectly obvious, but you can't get any constitutional lawyer to agree with you on them. It is perfectly obvious, for example, that if the three branches of government cannot agree to do something, it should not be done. That was the theory behind the Constitution. But no—we have to have someone supreme: the Court will make the ultimate decision.

And there is something else: secrecy in government. Secrecy in government exists for only one reason: to prevent the American people from knowing what's going on. It is nonsense to believe that anything our government does is not known to the Russians at about the moment it happens.

To me, the most ominous flaw in our constitutional setup is the fact that the federal government does not have control of money and credit and does not have control of corporations. It is therefore not really sovereign. And it is not really responsible, because it is now controlled by those two groups, corporations and those who control the flows of money. The new public financing of the presidential elections is arranged so that they can spend as much as they want: voluntary contributions, not authorized by the candidate, are legal.

The administrative system and elections are dominated

today by the private power of money flows and corporation activities. I want to read you a summary from James Willard Hurst, *The Legitimacy of the Business Corporation in the Law of the United States, 1780–1970* (Virginia, 1970). He points out that there was powerful anticorporation feeling in the United States in the 1820s. Therefore, it was established by the states that corporations could not exist by prescription; they had to have charters. They had to have a limited term of life and not be immortal. (Corporations today are immortal: if they get charters, they can live forever and bury us all.) They had to have a limited purpose. (Who is giving us this bread made of sawdust? ITT, International Telephone and Telegraph, the same corporation that drove Ivar Kreuger to suicide in Paris in April 1931, when it actually was an international telegraph corporation, controlled by J. P. Morgan.)

Hurst tells us further that in those nineteenth century days certain thin regulations were established in the United States regarding corporations: restricted purpose and activities, especially by banks and insurance companies; prohibition of one corporation's holding the stock of another without specific statutory grant; limits on the span of the life of a corporation, requiring recurrent legislative scrutiny; limits on total assets; limits on new issues of capital, so that the proportion of control of existing stockholders could be maintained; limits on the votes allowed to any stockholder, regardless of the size of his holding; and other such regulations.

By 1890 all of these had been destroyed by judicial interpretation, which extended to corporations—fictitious persons—those constitutional rights guaranteed, especially by the Fifteenth Amendment, to living persons. This interpretation was made possible by Roscoe Conklin, known as "Turkey Strut" Conklin, who told the Supreme Court that there were no records kept by the committee of the Senate that had drawn up the Fifteenth Amendment. But he had kept private notes which showed they had intended the word "person" to include corporations. It was most convenient. The corporation that was hiring him to do this suitably rewarded him.

The State of Individuals 1776–1976

Now I come to my last statement. I regret ending on what is, I suppose, such a pessimistic note—I am not personally pessimistic. In the end, the American people will ultimately prefer communities. They will cop out or opt out of the system. Today everything is a bureaucratic structure, and brainwashed people who are not personalities are trained to fit into this bureaucratic structure and say it is a great life—although I would assume that many on their death beds must feel otherwise.

The process of copping out will take a long time, but notice: we are already copping out of military service on a wholesale basis; we are already copping out of voting on a large scale. I heard an estimate tonight that the president will probably be chosen by forty percent of the people eligible to vote and that the percentage of voters who were registered but did not vote will be higher for the fourth time in sixteen years. People are also copping out by refusing to pay any attention to newspapers or to what's going on in the world, and by increasing emphasis on localism, what is happening in their own neighborhoods.

In this pathetic election, I am simply amazed that neither of the candidates has thought about such important issues as the rights of local areas to make their own decisions about those things affecting them. Now, I realize that if there's a sulphur mine or a sulphur factory a few miles away, localism is not much help. But I think you will find one extraordinary thing in this election: a considerable number of people will go to the polls and vote for the local candidates, but not for the president. That is the reverse of the situation fifty years ago.

But do not be pessimistic. Life goes on; life is fun. And if a civilization crashes it deserves to. When Rome fell, the Christian answer was, "Create our own communities."

CHAPTER 4

War and Peace in Soviet Diplomacy, 1939

JAN KARSKI

In his powerful work of historical scholarship, *The Great Powers and Poland, 1919–1945: From Versailles to Yalta* (University Press of America, 1985), Professor of Government Jan Karski documented his native Poland's inability to play, in his words, "an independent and effective role in the international arena." With what tragic consequences we are all too familiar. For his own activities during World War II and after, he received Poland's highest military decoration and was honored by the planting of a tree bearing his name in Jerusalem's Alley of the Righteous Gentiles among the Nations. This chapter from his book details the diplomacy of a pivotal year on the brink of calamity. It is an amazingly straightforward story of monumental treachery.

War and Peace in Soviet Diplomacy, 1939

WESTERN ALLIANCE OR GERMAN RAPPROCHEMENT?

After the destruction of Czechoslovakia's independence in March 1939, both Great Britain and France—finally recognizing that only force could stop Nazi expansion—approached the Soviet Union in hopes of creating a common front. They encountered a cautious reception and were asked for many clarifications. Because of the complex international situation in the spring and summer of 1939, Moscow had more than one possible course of action. Each possessed advantages and risks.

The Franco-British proposals aimed both at preventing Hitler from embarking upon new adventures and at securing Russia's military cooperation in the event Hitler continued his policy of conquest. Were Hitler confronted with the solidarity of great powers determined to defend any prospective victim, he might well reflect. In either case, the preservation of the status quo in central eastern Europe, particularly the protection of Poland and Rumania, was a basic feature of the early proposals.

The countries lying between Germany and Russia were strongly anti-Communist. In the past, all of them refused to conclude any mutual assistance pacts with Moscow; all of them feared and distrusted the Soviet Union. Their protection could hardly have been a goal in itself for the Kremlin, unless it offered some political or territorial gains. If demands for such gains were not approved by Paris and London, Moscow could refuse to join the proposed Franco-British defense system.

Such an act would not necessarily preclude French and British cooperation if Germany attacked the Soviet Union itself. Having no common frontier with Germany, Russia was already protected by the British-French guarantees to Poland and

Rumania. Before attacking Russia, Germany was likely to attack at least one of these countries first, thus automatically involving Great Britain and France in a war. There was no need, as far as the Soviet government was concerned, to assume new commitments in order to ensure British and French collaboration in case of war. On the contrary, it was the British and the French who, having already committed themselves, now needed Russia's commitments.

Moscow could refuse these commitments or assume them for a price. Would the Western democracies be willing to pay the price?

The Soviet position vis-à-vis Germany also offered opportunities. Hitler's decision to settle accounts with Poland had been evident since April 1939. Consequently, Russia's neutrality or cooperation was bound to be attractive to him. It would guarantee an easy victory and preclude a two-front war, which Hitler always wanted to avoid. How much was that neutrality worth to him, and what price would he be willing to pay?

The Soviet leaders certainly realized that their refusal to join the Western-initiated defense system could only encourage Hitler to continue his conquests. In view of the Franco-British obligations already assumed, this meant a war in which Germany would have to fight Great Britain and France. Such a war might also offer advantages to Moscow. The enemies of communism—Nazi Germany and the "bourgeois democracies"—would fight each other, while Russia, if it stayed out of the conflict, would preserve or even increase its strength. Was it not natural for the Soviet Union to stay out of such a war?

The Soviet leaders must have realized as well that if Germany attacked Poland and overran it, Russia's boundaries would become wide open to Nazi aggression. But was it inevitable that Hitler would then give orders to attack the Soviet Union? After all, this would mean opening a second front in his (they hoped) long and exhausting war against Great Britain and France.

Stalin Explores His Options. All these questions, and probably many others, had to be answered before the Soviet government

War and Peace in Soviet Diplomacy, 1939

made its decisions. To find the answers, Stalin, the undisputed steward of Soviet policies, began in the early spring of 1939 to engage in a double-decked, history-making diplomatic game.

On the one hand, he entered into discussions, both political and military, with the British and French in order to learn what they had to offer in return for Russia's cooperation. The issue was important and contained an inherent risk. Even if an agreement were reached and Germany were contained for the time being, Hitler would remain in power; he would still be able to maneuver; unpredictable fluctuations on the international scene would still be possible. Communist Russia did not have too many friends among the European government leaders, and the men in the Kremlin certainly realized that.

The Soviet government asked for a straight political alliance and for well-defined military commitments on the part of Great Britain and France. Furthermore, since Germany could attack Russia only through her Western neighbors—Finland, Estonia, Latvia, Poland, or Rumania—Moscow asked for special rights, not necessarily dependent on those neighbors' approval. In the event they were threatened by Germany, or their policies reoriented in a way contrary to Russia's interests, Moscow asked for permission to take necessary military measures in order to "protect" them for the sake of Russia's own security. For all practical purposes, Moscow requested recognition of a security zone comprising territory from Finland to Rumania.

Simultaneously, and in the greatest secrecy, Stalin initiated negotiations with the Nazis, trying to determine what price Hitler was willing to pay for Russia's neutrality in his intended attack on Poland.

It eventually became clear that the Western powers, though ready to conclude an alliance with Russia, were in no position to assume military commitments commensurate with the war effort expected of the Soviet Union if Germany moved eastward.[1] Until very late, they were also more interested in preserving the status quo than in recognizing Russia's "special interests" in central eastern Europe. Not surprisingly, all countries from Finland to Rumania registered their opposition to such a recognition.

Jan Karski

It was different with the Nazis. Not only did Hitler, after some hesitation, accept Moscow's request for an understanding, but ultimately he agreed to pay for Russia's neutrality by recognizing large areas in Eastern Europe as a Soviet sphere of interest. This evidently determined the course of Soviet diplomacy. It also made a Nazi attack on Poland inevitable.

Stalin's first public, though cryptic, initiative for an understanding with Germany took place on March 10, just a few days before the Nazi seizure of Prague. In a speech to the Eighteenth Congress of the All-Union Communist Party held in Moscow, he described the situation in Europe, sharply criticizing the policy of the Western powers, which had substituted for the concept of "collective security" a policy of "nonintervention." The goal of their new policy, he sarcastically observed, was not an attempt to stop Fascist expansion, but rather to direct it away from themselves.

The speech was markedly conciliatory toward Germany. Stalin showed readiness to develop economic relations with the Reich and said that he did not believe Germany planned to seize the Ukraine, in spite of the "hullabaloo raised by the British, French, and American press." He noted that "it looks as if the object of this suspicious hullabaloo was to incense the Soviet Union against Germany, to poison the atmosphere and to provoke a conflict with Germany without any visible grounds." The Communist party, he concluded, "would not allow" Russia "to be drawn into conflicts by warmongers who are accustomed to get others to pull the chestnuts out of the fire for them." He even suggested that the anti-Comintern pact was directed against the Western democracies rather than against the Soviet Union.[2] The Congress's deliberations were followed by attacks on France and Great Britain in the Soviet press.

The Franco-British Approaches

The first Franco-British attempt to establish cooperation with Russia took place three days after the Nazi occupation of Czechoslovakia and amidst rumors that Rumania was in dan-

War and Peace in Soviet Diplomacy, 1939

ger. On March 18 Lord Halifax, the British foreign secretary, proposed that France, the Soviet Union, and Poland join Britain in a public declaration of mutual understanding, in case of a "threat to the political independence of any European state." The French government agreed without delay. The Soviets agreed in principle, asking that the Baltic, Balkan, and Scandinavian states participate in the declaration. They also suggested that an Anglo-Franco-Rumanian-Soviet conference be summoned first, preferably in Bucharest.[3]

But, Poland opposed the plan. So did Rumania.[4] And the British initiative came to naught.

Although French foreign minister Georges Bonnet shared apprehensions over Soviet foreign policy, he was determined to bring Russia into the anti-Nazi defense system at any cost. He wanted, first, to conclude a direct Soviet-French military agreement and, second, to secure direct Soviet aid for the East European countries, even against those countries' own wishes, in case of German aggression. Only Moscow's agreement on both points, he reasoned, could make operative the Franco-Soviet pact of mutual assistance (concluded in 1935).[5]

As to the first point, on April 5 the Quai d'Orsay proposed immediate negotiations on the subject of a military convention. Moscow did not refuse but demanded that Great Britain assume the same obligations toward the Soviet Union that France had already assumed or would do in the future. As to the second point, Bonnet proposed an agreement that would have the U.S.S.R. assist Poland and Rumania in case of war. Since both of them refused to enter into any mutual assistance pacts with Russia, he suggested that the agreement, as well as the negotiations, be kept secret.[6]

The suggestion blatantly disregarded the stipulations of the Franco-Polish alliance prohibiting such dealings. But the stakes were high and the danger imminent. Besides, by that time, Poland's position in Paris was low and the policies of its foreign minister, Col. Józef Beck, were generally held in disrepute. Obviously the Quai d'Orsay did not feel bound by the terms of the alliance.

Jan Karski

In London's governmental circles, Polish and Rumanian opposition to any military collaboration with Russia aroused more understanding than in Paris. But the cabinet felt that the impasse had to be broken. By then a most disquieting message came from the British ambassador in Moscow, Sir William Seeds. Seeds felt that the attitude of Poland and Rumania might push Russia into an isolationist, neutral position. The Soviet leaders, he reasoned, were pretty sure that if Germany attacked Poland or Rumania, Great Britain and France would go to war regardless of Moscow's attitude. But then, he argued, they might hope that even if Germany overran those countries, Hitler would have no interest in attacking Russia and increasing the number of his enemies. Thus, Moscow had reason to feel relatively safe. Furthermore, once the war broke out, the Soviets could engage in a "profitable business" of selling supplies. Ambassador Seeds urged that pressure be brought upon Poland and Rumania to enter into a military cooperation with Russia as soon as possible and certainly *before* the war started.[7]

By the time Seeds's message reached London on April 14, the Foreign Office had already dispatched a new proposal to Moscow—a unilateral Soviet guarantee similar to the British and French guarantees. In the event of aggression against any of Russia's European neighbors that the victim resisted militarily, the assistance of the Soviet Union would be available *if desired*.[8] The proposal took cognizance of Warsaw's and Bucharest's objections and was agreeable to both.

Moves and Countermoves. The Soviet counterproposals, put forth on April 18, deepened the impasse. First, Moscow asked that Russia's northwestern neighbors—Finland, Estonia, and Latvia—be covered by the same guarantees as Poland and Rumania. Germany might try to expand into that region, it was argued, and thus directly threaten the Soviet Union. The Soviet government, for its own sake, had a duty to protect those countries.

Then Great Britain, France, and Russia would have to conclude a mutual assistance pact. In the event of a German attack against any of the countries covered by the guarantees, the signatories of the pact would bring all aid, including military, to the victim of aggression. The form, extent, and circumstances of that aid were not specified; and, more important, again it was to be given regardless of whether the "protected" countries wanted it or not.

Ominously, the Soviet government also asked London to inform Warsaw formally that British guarantees were meant to cover *only German* aggression. Moreover, Poland and Rumania were either to declare their own mutual assistance pact, covering the eventuality of Soviet aggression, as null and void, or to make that pact cover any—not only Soviet—aggression.[9]

Although Moscow's proposals had no chance of being approved voluntarily by any of Russia's neighbors, the French decided to accept them, considering agreement with Moscow absolutely necessary. But the British dissented, mainly in consideration of the opposition offered by Poland.[10] Some new solutions had to be devised.

Ten days later, on April 28, Halifax presented a new formula that seemed to solve the difficulties. He suggested that Russia, on its own initiative, declare unilaterally that it would render assistance to Great Britain and France if they became involved in a war on account of their previous public guarantees. Neither Poland nor Rumania would be mentioned directly, although in the event of war the declaration would obviously affect them.

Warsaw approved the formula, which left Poland free to decide whether to cooperate with Russia if war actually broke out.[11] Moscow, however, rejected it on May 15, arguing that it did not provide for reciprocity and did not cover the Baltic states.[12]

Although key British government officials did show an understanding of Colonel Beck's apprehensions and objections, by then many were criticizing the Poles. Lloyd George and Churchill, in particular, disapproved of Poland's fears and distrust of Russia and raised their voices in the House of Commons. On May 4 Churchill gave vent to his disappointment over the delay in the British-French-Soviet negotiations by observing that Britain and France had a right "to call upon Poland not to place obstacles in the way of common cause." He urged rapid conclusion of a pact with Moscow. "There is no means of maintaining an Eastern Front against Nazi aggression without the active aid of Russia," he warned.[13]

MOSCOW'S DOUBLE-DEALING

Simultaneously with Soviet foreign minister Maksim Litvinov's proposal of the triple Anglo-French-Soviet military alliance, German secretary of state Baron Ernest von Weizsaecker was "enigmatically" approached on April 17 by the Soviet ambassador, Alexei Merekalov.

Merekalov reportedly observed that "ideological differences of opinion had hardly influenced the Russian-Italian relationship, and they did not have to prove a stumbling block with regard to Germany either. Soviet Russia had not exploited the present friction between Germany and the Western democracies against [Germany], nor did she desire to do so. There exist[ed] for Russia no reason why she should not live with [Germany] on a normal footing. And, from normal, the relations might become better and better."[14]

Merekalov's declaration, the significance of which Weizsaecker duly reported, produced immediate and noticeable results. The Nazi press stopped its attacks on the U.S.S.R. Even more striking, in a speech on April 28 Hitler failed to denounce communism, probably for the first time in his public career.

A few days later Moscow took a further step. Litvinov—a "champion" of collective security and British-Franco-Soviet anti-Nazi cooperation, and also a Jew—was dismissed on May 3. His successor was Vyacheslav Molotov, a powerful member of the Politburo who enjoyed a reputation as a Soviet "nationalist."

Two days later Georgi Astakhov, counselor at the Soviet embassy in Berlin, called on Dr. Karl Schnurre of the Auswärtiges Amt [Foreign Office] to inquire whether the new nomination "would cause a change in Germany's attitude toward the Soviet Union." Astakhov approached Schnurre again on May 17 and cautiously commented that "there was no reason for enmity" between Germany and Russia. He referred

War and Peace in Soviet Diplomacy, 1939

specifically to the Rapallo treaty of 1922 and pointedly expressed skepticism about the Anglo-Franco-Soviet negotiations. Molotov went even further three days later. In his conversation with the German ambassador in Moscow, Count Werner von der Schulenburg, he applied some pressure, observing that the "Soviet Government could only agree to resumption of [economic] negotiations if the necessary 'political basis' for them had been found."

Molotov was vague and cautious, but Schulenburg easily caught the meaning of the observation and reported to Berlin that "it cannot be understood otherwise than that the resumption of our [German-Soviet] economic negotiations does not satisfy [Molotov] as a political gesture and that he apparently wants to obtain from us more extensive proposals of a political nature." Molotov's initiative surprised Schulenburg, who recommended that Berlin proceed with "extreme caution." Hitler agreed and instructed his ambassador in Moscow to be careful and to wait for the Soviet side to make more specific proposals.[15]

In the meantime, Anglo-French-Soviet negotiations continued; in Paris and London it seemed as if some progress was being made. Initially the British wanted to avoid a direct alliance with Russia, trying instead to commit Moscow to the defense of Germany's neighbors and prospective victims only. Hard-pressed by the French, London eventually gave its basic approval to Moscow's proposals of April 18.

The British and the French governments both agreed to come to Russia's assistance in case of either a direct German attack or a war resulting from Russia's aid to a victim of German aggression. Their only condition was that Russia's aid to any country covered by the guarantees would have to be agreed upon by that country or, in the case of a neutral country, would come in response to an appeal for aid.[16] Although the formulation of the draft did not respond entirely to Moscow's demands, both London and Paris were optimistic as to Soviet reaction.

At that time, Hitler was still uncertain whether Germany's policy toward Russia should be reoriented and, if so, to what extent. But he realized the portentous significance of the Anglo-

French-Soviet negotiations. An alliance among those three powers would mean an effective encirclement of Germany and frustration of his decision to break Poland. An alliance among Great Britain, France, and Russia might also preclude any future expansion of Germany. Hitler apparently concluded that only some immediate initiative on his part might prevent Moscow from joining the Western powers. The matter seemed urgent because, on May 24, Chamberlain announced that an agreement between Great Britain and the Soviet Union was imminent.

Three days after the Franco-British draft was forwarded to Moscow—on May 30—Weizsaecker summoned Astakhov and told him that if the Soviet government responded to the British "enticements," any normalization of German-Soviet relations would become impossible. He hinted at such a normalization and assured the Soviet diplomat that Germany had no designs on the Ukraine. The rumors to the contrary were due to Beck's intrigues and his personal "interpretation" of German plans and policies. He pointed out that Germany's agreement to the incorporation of Carpatho-Ukraine by Hungary represented the best "refutation" of suspicions that Berlin wanted to play the Ukrainian card against Russia. And, because of the recent strain on German-Polish relations, he observed, Berlin now had more freedom of action against Poland.[17]

The Soviet reaction was instantaneous. The following day, Molotov, in his public report to the Supreme Soviet, sharply criticized negotiations with Great Britain and France and emphasized Moscow's right to conclude an economic agreement with Berlin.[18] Even more important, he also raised new issues in his negotiations with the British and the French.

On June 2 the Soviet government formally proposed its own draft treaty with France and Great Britain. It provided for mutual assistance in the event any of the three were directly attacked or were involved in war resulting from "aggression" against Belgium, Greece, Turkey, Rumania, Poland, Latvia, Estonia, or Finland. The "assistance" given to any of these countries would not be conditioned either by their agreement

War and Peace in Soviet Diplomacy, 1939

to or request for it. The treaty would not take effect until a special agreement specifying the extent of each signatory's military contribution was also concluded.[19]

The proposals, if accepted, would give Russia a right, in the event of war, to occupy any of her neighboring states under the pretext of protecting it from aggression. That such might be the result all Russia's neighbors were strongly convinced, and when informed about Molotov's proposals, all registered their opposition. Warsaw did so through the Polish ambassador in London, Count Edward Raczynski, on June 10, as did the representatives of Latvia, Estonia, Finland, and Rumania.[20] French premier Edouard Daladier himself did not hesitate to raise the issue bluntly with the Soviet ambassador in Paris. Both the Quai d'Orsay and the Foreign Office understood the Soviet proposals as a formal demand for a free hand in central eastern Europe.[21]

During that time, Nazi anti-Polish war propaganda reached its peak, indicating that Franco-British commitments vis-à-vis Poland did not suffice to make Hitler pause. It was becoming more and more obvious that only Russia's immediate adherence to the Western system of defense might deter Nazi Germany from starting a war. Anxious to secure this adherence, the British government decided to send a special envoy, Sir William Strang, to Moscow.

Strang arrived in Moscow on June 14 and tortuous negotiations resumed. On June 16 Molotov proposed a new alternative, which was mainly a straight defensive alliance between the three powers, providing for mutual assistance but only in the event of *direct* aggression against any one of them.[22] This ran against the entire Franco-British policy. The whole idea of the negotiations was to commit Russia to the defense of Germany's neighbors. Hitler had to be convinced that in the event of Germany's aggression against *any* country, Russia, Great Britain, and France would go to war jointly. Informed of the proposal, Halifax declined to consider it "except in the last resort."[23]

By then it became evident to the Western leaders that without serious concessions, the Soviet government would not join an anti-Nazi coalition. As a result, on June 27, new instructions were sent to Ambassador Seeds. Soviet terms for assistance to be accorded to all "guaranteed" countries were accepted. Halifax had only two wishes—namely, that the Netherlands and Switzerland also be "guaranteed," and that the list of guaranteed countries be kept secret. He feared that some of them might embarrass the signatories by publicly disassociating themselves from the "guarantors." This might easily have been the case with any of Russia's neighbors. Molotov was informed about the suggestions from the British and French ambassadors on July 1.[24]

Molotov's reaction surprised the ambassadors. Unexpectedly, he raised a new demand. "Indirect" aggression should also entitle the "guarantors" to give "assistance." Two days later, on July 3, an official Soviet note specified that "an internal coup d'état or a reversal of policy in the interests of the aggressor" would have to be considered an "indirect aggression." This definition, the note emphasized, should apply to all "guaranteed" countries: Estonia, Latvia, Finland, Poland, Rumania, Turkey, Greece, and Belgium. The note rejected the proposal to extend the guarantee to the Netherlands and Switzerland, unless Poland and Turkey agreed to conclude mutual assistance pacts with the Soviet Union.[25]

The acceptance of the Soviet proposal would give Russia a right to "assist" any of her neighbors under practically any circumstances, even in peacetime, regardless of the wish of the country concerned. Any change of, say, a cabinet minister, might be interpreted by Moscow as being "in the interest of the aggressor," with the Red Army occupying the territory in order to bring "assistance." The British, realizing that the countries concerned would never approve of such an arrangement—and by now more strongly than ever distrusting Moscow's motives—reluctantly declined. The negotiations nevertheless continued, in no small measure due to the insistence of the French. Daladier was firmly convinced that only an alliance among Great Britain, France, and Russia, and the latter's commitment of support in the event of Germany's aggression against Poland or any other country, could deter Hitler from war. So was Bonnet,

War and Peace in Soviet Diplomacy, 1939

who sent a personal message to Halifax, dated July 19, urging him to conclude an agreement with Russia on whatever terms.[26]

Toying with Poland. While forging ever closer links with the Auswärtiges Amt and simultaneously upping the price for Russia's cooperation with the Western democracies, the Soviet Foreign Ministry, the Narkomindel, did not neglect Poland. On May 7 Molotov congratulated the Polish ambassador in Moscow, Waclaw Grzybowski, on Beck's May 5 speech. He "especially emphasized how much he had been impressed by [Beck's] words on national honor."[27] Three days later, Vladimir Potemkin, deputy commissar for foreign affairs, visited Warsaw and—according to a special circular sent by Beck to all Polish diplomatic missions abroad—assured the Poles that the Soviet leaders were ready to support Poland on Warsaw's conditions:

> The Soviets realize that the Polish Government is not prepared to enter any agreement with either one of Poland's great neighbors against the other and understand the advantages to them of this attitude. . . .
>
> Mr. Potemkin also stated that in the event of an armed conflict between Poland and Germany, the Soviets will adopt *une attitude bienveillante* toward [Poland].
>
> As Mr. Potemkin himself later indicated, his statements were made in accordance with special instructions which the Soviet government had sent to Warsaw for him.[28]

Following Potemkin's declaration in Warsaw, the Soviet officials continued to demonstrate their willingness to help Poland in the event of German aggression. There were vague suggestions that Russia might supply Poland with arms. True, a formal agreement on conditions never materialized, but goodwill seemed to be there. On May 31 Molotov included in his report to the Supreme Soviet a paragraph referring to Poland in warm and friendly terms. He referred approvingly to the Polish-Soviet communiqué of November 26, 1938, as

Jan Karski

"confirming the development of good neighborly relations between the USSR and Poland" and concluded by emphasizing "all-around improvement" in Polish-Soviet relations.[29] Two days later, on June 2, a similar declaration was made by the newly appointed Soviet ambassador in Warsaw.

As a result, Beck instructed Grzybowski to seek a special agreement in Moscow for the passage of Western supplies in the event of German attack. Again, although publicly the Soviet government denied committing itself to supply Poland with raw materials in case of war, *secretly* Potemkin assured the Polish ambassador that once Poland *actually* found herself in war, everything would probably change and Moscow would give permission for the transit.[30]

Back on the Nazi Track. While the Franco-British-Soviet negotiations were dragging in Moscow, the supersecret Nazi-Soviet contacts in Berlin were taking more and more concrete shape. On June 14, the day Strang arrived in Moscow, Astakhov let the Nazi authorities know through the Bulgarian minister in Berlin that if Germany concluded a nonaggression pact with Russia, the Soviet government "would probably refrain from concluding a treaty with England." Three days later, Astakhov told Schulenburg, who was passing through Berlin, that good German-Soviet relations served both countries well in the past. "The whole course of history had shown that Germany and Russia had always done well when they had been friends, and badly when they had been enemies," he said. Hitler, however, was still hesitant. As late as June 30 instructions were sent to Schulenburg to be noncommittal. But he was also informed that Berlin considered it "important" that Moscow "had taken the initiative for the rapprochement."[31]

Hitler made up his mind soon afterward. In the second part of July his military command submitted the final plans for an attack against Poland. The attack, if executed in 1939, had to be mounted in a matter of weeks. The usual fall rains might make many Polish areas inaccessible to mechanized divisions. Thus, Russia's neutrality, essential all along, now became urgent. Furthermore, Hitler must have feared that Franco-

War and Peace in Soviet Diplomacy, 1939

British-Soviet negotiations might still produce some understanding, impeding all his plans. From mid-July on, it was Hitler who would press for a Nazi-Soviet agreement to be concluded as speedily as possible.

On July 22 Schulenburg received instructions "to pick up the threads again." Four days later, in Berlin, Schnurre told Astakhov that the interests of the German and Soviet policies did not conflict and their ideological differences were balanced by their mutual opposition to capitalist democracies. He warned against Russia's understanding with Britain, suggested a full-fledged agreement, and clearly indicated that Berlin was ready to pay a price for it:

> What could England offer Russia? At best, participation in a European war and the hostility of Germany, but not a single desirable end for Russia.
>
> What could we offer on the other hand? Neutrality and staying out of a possible European conflict and, if Moscow wishes, a German-Russian understanding on mutual interest, which, just as in former times, would work out to the advantage of both countries.[32]

This time Astakhov answered without even asking for time to receive instructions. He unhesitatingly indicated Soviet interest in the Baltic countries, in Finland, and in Rumania. He inquired cautiously if Germany had any interest in Polish Galicia. Casually, he asked if Germany had any designs on the Ukraine. Schnurre vehemently denied any such interest or designs; and as for the areas enumerated by Astakhov, he assured the Soviet diplomat that Germany would present no obstacles.

Three days later, on July 29, Schulenburg was ordered to inform Molotov officially that Germany recognized Russia's "vital interests" in Poland and the Baltic states. German foreign minister Joachim von Ribbentrop made a similar declaration to the Soviet chargé d'affaires in Berlin on August 2. Ribbentrop mentioned that in case of war with Poland, the latter would be crushed in a week. Therefore, he suggested a German-Soviet understanding on the future of Poland.

Jan Karski

On August 10 Schnurre bluntly asked Astakhov what exactly Soviet interests in Poland were. This time, Astakhov refused to give the answer without specific instructions. Two days later he informed Schnurre that the Soviet government would like to discuss the Polish problem, as well as others, and proposed Moscow as the place for negotiations.[33] Informed about the conversation, Schulenburg advised that Ribbentrop go to Moscow immediately.

Molotov received the offer of Ribbentrop's visit with "interest" and "warm welcome," but he did not seem to be in any hurry. Such a visit, he argued, had to be prepared. First, preliminary negotiations had to be concluded so that "concrete decisions" could be made when the German foreign minister came to Moscow.[34] Was Stalin afraid of some trap? Did he still want to continue the negotiations with the French and British missions? Was he still weighing Western and Nazi concessions, making time with both?

Endless Soviet Demands. In the third week of July it seemed to Paris and London that the Franco-British-Soviet negotiations were about to be successfully concluded in Moscow. On July 23 the British and French ambassadors formally informed Molotov that their governments agreed to simultaneous conclusion of political and military pacts. The Soviet demand for the unconditional right to protect "guaranteed" countries in the event not only of "direct" but of "indirect" aggression was accepted.

The only demand Paris and London made was for a formula of "assistance" that would preclude "interference in internal affairs" of any given country. The countries covered by the guarantees were to be enumerated in a special protocol; all Russia's western neighbors would be included, in addition to Greece, Turkey, and Belgium. The protocol was to be *secret* so that the "guaranteed" countries would not be exposed to Hitler's wrath. Thus, after several months of negotiations, Moscow's demands—all of them—were approved.[35]

When the French and British representatives made their declaration, the Soviet leaders were still awaiting Hitler's final

War and Peace in Soviet Diplomacy, 1939

answer to their proposals for an agreement. This might have been responsible for Molotov's reaction, because he still demurred. The Soviet government, he said, could not sign the agreement before the military convention was worked out in all details. Paris and London had no choice but to dispatch their military representatives—Gen. Joseph Doumenc and Adm. Sir Reginald Plunkett-Drax, respectively. They arrived in Moscow on August 11—an unfortunate delay under the circumstances.

Three days after their arrival, Marshal Clementi Voroshilov, representing the Red Army, confronted them with demands never before advanced and which created a new situation. In the event of war, the Red Army would have to occupy the main islands and ports of the Baltic states and have free passage through Poland and Rumania. In Poland, he specified, the Red Army would have to occupy Lvov and Vilna. It was up to the French and British governments to obtain formal consent from the countries in question. The Red Army could not watch passively while those countries were being destroyed by Germany just because their governments were unwilling to ask for Soviet aid, he explained.[36]

As Voroshilov was making the declaration, the foundation for the Nazi-Soviet agreement had already been laid down and Ribbentrop's visit to Moscow already decided upon. Neither the French nor the British governments had any way of knowing that for Russia's cooperation Stalin was now demanding from them virtually the same price he already knew Hitler would pay, namely, approval of Soviet expansion into the Baltic states, eastern Poland, and Rumania.

Did that mean that Stalin still wanted to have alternatives? That if his new demands were approved, there was still a possibility, even at such a late hour, that Russia might accede to the Western system of defense? Without access to the Kremlin's archives, no answer could be offered.

By August, it became evident to the Western leaders that some sort of a dramatic showdown was near unless the new Soviet demands were met. Both the French and British ambassadors in Moscow considered those demands "justified" and strongly advised pressing the Poles and the Rumanians for their assent. Without delay, appropriate instructions were sent to the French and British ambassadors in Warsaw, Leon Noël and Howard Kennard, and without delay they contacted the Polish authorities, arguing that to leave such an important matter as Soviet military aid to the negotiations *after* the German attack would be futile.[37]

The Poles were immovable. Poland's acceptance of Moscow's demands, argued Beck, would probably provoke Germany into a war "immediately." He did not exclude the possibility that Voroshilov's request might even be a provocation. If Poland agreed, the Soviets would probably inform Hitler about it themselves. Besides, he was not convinced at all that once the Red Army occupied the eastern part of Poland, Russia would fight Germany. "This is a new partition which we are asked to sign; if we are to be partitioned, we shall at least defend ourselves," he told Noël. The Poles had no doubt that once the Red Army entered their country, communism would be imposed. "With the Germans we are risking our freedom. With the Russians we lose our soul,"[38] said Marshal Edward Smigly-Rydz, head of Poland's armed forces.

Warsaw's stand evoked bitter criticism, particularly in Paris. Daladier considered it a folly. As he angrily told U.S. Ambassador to Moscow William C. Bullitt on August 18, the Soviet demands were justified and bona fide. He understood that the Poles were reluctant to have the Red Army on their territories. But he also considered that once Poland had been attacked by Germany, the Poles should be happy to have anyone's assistance. France could guarantee that the Soviet forces would eventually evacuate Poland. Besides, both France and Great Britain could send some of their own land forces to Poland so that there would be an international, not just a Soviet, contingent there. Daladier seemed extremely excited and frustrated. He repeated three times that should the Poles persist in rejecting the Soviet offer, he would not send a "single peasant" to die in defense of Poland.[39]

The next day, August 19, Bonnet instructed Noël to tell Beck that France as an ally had a right to ask just how Poland proposed to resist Germany without Russia's help. Beck's fre-

War and Peace in Soviet Diplomacy, 1939

quently expressed wish for the successful conclusion of the Anglo-Franco-Soviet negotiations was misleading, he argued, since evidently Poland's refusal to cooperate with Russia precluded any possibility of success from the very beginning. He urged Noël to do his best in order to secure some formula for a Polish-Soviet military cooperation. Noël's intervention resulted in a complete fiasco.[40]

The day the Anglo-French-Soviet military discussions started, August 12, the Auswärtiges Amt received information that Molotov was ready to discuss all questions, Poland's future included. Two days later Schulenburg received detailed instructions to solemnly inform the Soviet government that Germany would agree to settle all questions "between the Baltic Sea and the Black Sea" to the "complete satisfaction" of both countries, and that "German-Russian policy . . . has come to an historic turning point."

On August 16 Ribbentrop asked for an immediate meeting with Stalin and Molotov. Only three days later, the Soviet draft of the pact was dispatched to Berlin. The next day, the approval, accompanied by Hitler's personal message to Stalin, was sent to Moscow. In answer, Stalin thanked Hitler for the "assent of the German Government to the conclusion of a nonaggression pact."[41] The next day, August 22, Ribbentrop's visit to Moscow was announced publicly. Hitler summoned his commanders the same day to discuss the attack on Poland, which he scheduled for August 26.

Frantic Moves and Failure. The public announcement of Ribbentrop's trip to Moscow fell upon Europe like a bombshell. The same day Bonnet instructed Noël to ask Beck for Poland's "sacrifice." Warsaw, the instruction ran, should immediately give General Doumenc in Moscow *carte blanche* as to its approval of the passage of the Soviet troops through Poland. Otherwise the responsibility for the failure of Franco-British-Soviet negotiations would fall on the Poles. On Paris's request, Kennard received instructions to support Noël in his dramatic representation.[42] Of course, neither the French nor the British knew for certain that the Nazi-Soviet agreement had been decided and that the destruction of Poland and the Baltic states as well as the partition of Rumania virtually agreed upon. The joint Noël-Kennard representation made in Warsaw failed. Although this time Beck did not exclude the "possibility" of the German-Soviet agreement "for a partition of Poland," he refused to yield. Realizing the gravity of the situation, he did agree, however, to a carefully phrased formula. General Doumenc was authorized to declare in Moscow that the French government had "learned for certain that in the event of common action against German aggression, collaboration, under technical conditions to be settled subsequently between Poland and the U.S.S.R. [was] not excluded."[43]

The hour was late, and in a frantic attempt to keep Russia away from Germany, Paris went far beyond Beck's authorization. That very evening, General Doumenc, acting under instructions, formally declared to Voroshilov that France was ready to sign an agreement to the Soviet request for military passage through Poland. The declaration was never authorized by Warsaw. Nor was it sponsored by the British government. Nor did it produce any positive results. It was not France's approval, but Poland's that was sought, answered Voroshilov, and on this note the discussion ended.[44]

A few hours later the Nazi-Soviet pact was signed. Two days later, on August 25, Molotov officially terminated the Franco-British-Soviet negotiations.

Stalin's Pact with Hitler

The Nazi-Soviet pact, signed in the late hours of August 23 in Moscow by Ribbentrop and Molotov, was a mutual commitment to nonaggression. According to article I, in case one party was involved in a military conflict, the other party was to maintain neutrality. The usual formula used in nonaggression pacts—namely, "unprovoked aggression"—was significantly omitted. Regardless of whether one party *was attacked* or *committed an act of aggression*, the other signatory was to remain neutral. Article III stipulated that each government would consult with the other on mutually important problems.

Article IV stipulated that the signatories would not partici-

War and Peace in Soviet Diplomacy, 1939

pate "in any grouping of Powers whatsoever that is directly or indirectly aimed at the other Party." It was this provision that bound the Soviet Union to break the negotiations with Great Britain and France. They "aimed" at Germany. The pact was concluded for ten years and entered into force at the moment of its signing.

For all practical purposes, the agreement was a pact of aggression. The secret protocol divided Eastern Europe into two "spheres of interest," and its provisions directly concerned Finland, Latvia, Lithuania, Estonia, Poland, and Rumania. Any political and territorial changes were to be effected by mutual accord. Finland, Latvia, Estonia, the eastern half of Poland, and Bessarabia were recognized as the Soviet sphere. The western half of Poland and all of Lithuania were assigned to Germany.[45]

As soon as the agreement was signed, a champagne party in honor of Ribbentrop took place at the Kremlin. It was marked by a feeling of triumph and mutual satisfaction. "It has been Stalin who through his speech in March of this year, which had been well understood in Germany, has brought about the reversal in [Nazi-Soviet] political relations," Molotov solemnly declared.[46] As for Stalin, he addressed himself directly to his peer in Berlin and proposed a toast to the Führer.

Soviet diplomacy continued to play its role to the end: Soviet efforts to strengthen Polish opposition to German demands continued even after the conclusion of the Nazi-Soviet pact. On August 24 Sharonov, the Soviet ambassador to Poland, assured Beck that the Nazi-Soviet pact would not change the attitude of the Soviet government toward Poland. On August 27, three days before the German attack and just three weeks before the Red Army invaded Poland, *Izvestya* published an interview with Voroshilov. The highest-ranking Soviet military officer suggested that it was possible for the Soviet Union to deliver raw materials and even military equipment to Poland and that no special agreement of mutual assistance or military convention was necessary for that purpose.

On September 2, while German panzer divisions were already rolling into Poland, Sharonov called upon Beck and asked why the Polish government failed to negotiate with Moscow the matter of Soviet supplies, as the "Voroshilov interview had opened up the possibility of getting them." As late as September 11, just six days before the Red Army marched into Poland, Sharonov was still discussing with the Polish under secretary of state, Count Jan Szembek, the problem of medical supplies from the Soviet Union. Sharanov discounted the rumors about Soviet mobilization of troops.[47]

Stalin's diplomacy enabled Hitler to start a war in which Nazi Germany on the one side and the "bourgeois democracies" on the other were to fight, while Russia stood to the side, unscathed and well rewarded for its neutrality. "If those gentlemen have such an uncontrollable desire to fight, let them do their fighting without the Soviet Union. We shall see what fighting stuff they are made of," chuckled Molotov to the Supreme Soviet a few hours before the war started. As *Izvestya* reported on September 1, 1939, the audience answered with laughter and applause.

It was a hollow victory. The laughter preceded the agony and death of 20 million Soviet citizens by only twenty-two months.

On that September day in 1939 Hitler must have felt that, against all odds, the hand of Providence was still guiding his steps toward his final goal—the destruction of Russia. The attainment of that goal had always depended on the Polish corridor to Russia being opened to him. Now he was to open that corridor by war and with Russia's help. In his dreams, Germany's victory would be bought cheaply. Then, Russia's turn would come and the indestructible foundations for his Thousand-Year Reich would finally be laid down.

"Now I have the whole world in my pocket," Hitler shouted deliriously upon receiving the news that Stalin agreed to speed up the conclusion of the pact.[48] The Great Vandal had his Great Day.

War and Peace in Soviet Diplomacy, 1939

ENDNOTES

1. For the minutes of the Franco-British-Soviet military negotiations in Moscow, see Ernest Llewellyn Woodward and Rohan Butler (eds.), *Documents on British Foreign Policy [hereafter DBFP], 1919–1939* (London: H.M. Stationery Office 1946–1955), 3rd series (9 vols. for the years 1930–1939), VII, pp. 558–614.

2. Jane Degras (ed.), *Soviet Documents on Foreign Policy, 1917–1941*, 3 vols. (London: Oxford University Press, 1951–1953), III, pp. 319–23.

3. *DBFP*, 3rd Series, IV, pp. 400, 490–91, 467.

4. Ibid., pp. 578–79; also V, pp. 312–13.

5. See the minutes of his conference in London on March 21, 1939; *DBFP*, 3rd Series, IV, pp. 422–27.

6. Georges Bonnet, *Défense de la paix*, 2 vols. (Genève: Les Editions du Cheval Ailé, 1946–1948), II, pp. 176–80, 190; see also *DBFP*, 3rd Series, V, p. 216.

7. *DBFP*, 3rd Series, V, p. 104.

8. Ibid., pp. 205–6; also Lord Strang, *Home and Abroad* (London: Andre Deutsch, 1956) pp. 162–63.

9. *DBFP*, 3rd Series, V, pp. 228–29; also Bonnet, *Défense de la paix*, II, p. 182. For the text of the proposals: Degras, *Soviet Documents*, III, p. 329.

10. *DBFP*, 3rd Series, V, p. 268; see also Bonnet, *Défense de la paix*, II, pp. 186–87.

11. *DBFP*, 3rd Series, V, pp. 357, 378.

12. For the text of the Soviet note, see Degras, *Soviet Documents*, III, pp. 330–31.

13. Winston S. Churchill, *The Gathering Storm* (Boston: Houghton Mifflin, 1948), p. 365.

14. Department of State, *Documents on German Foreign Policy* [hereafter *DGFP*], Series D, vols. II–VII (Washington, D.C.: U.S. Government Printing Office, 1957), VI, pp.266–67.

15. Ibid., pp. 429, 536, 547, 558, respectively.

16. Strang, *Home and Abroad*, pp. 167–68.

17. *DGFP*, Series D, VI, pp. 604–9.

18. Degras, *Soviet Documents*, III, p. 337.

19. *DBFP*, 3rd Series, V, pp. 753–54.

20. Ibid., VI, pp. 24–25, 48–49, 95–96, 120–22; V, pp. 746–47 respectively.

21. Strang, *Home and Abroad*, pp. 168–69; for Bullitt's report on Bonnet's and Daladier's opinion, Department of State, *Foreign Relations of the United States* [hereafter *FRUS*], (Washington, D.C.: U.S. Government Printing Office), 1939, I, pp. 266–70.

22. Degras, *Soviet Documents*, III, p. 349.

23. *DBFP*, 3rd Series, VI, pp. 103–5.

24. Ibid., pp. 173–74.

25. Ibid., pp. 230–32, 251–52, 313, 450–51.

26. Ibid., pp. 396–98; also Assemblé Nationale, *Les événements survenus en France de 1933 à 1945*, 9 vols. (Paris: Imprimerie Nationale, 1947–1951), IX, pp. 2669–74 (Bonnet's testimony).

JAN KARSKI

27 Republic of Poland, *The Polish White Book: Official Documents Concerning Polish-German and Polish-Soviet Relations* [hereafter *PWB*], (London: Hutchison Co., 1940), p. 208.
28 *PWB*, p. 183; also *DBFP*, 3rd Series, V, p. 657.
29 *Supra*, p. 351.
30 Degras, *Soviet Documents*, III, pp. 327, 328, *PWB*, 184, 208, respectively.
31 *DGFP*, Series D, VI, pp. 729, 741–42, 813, 911, respectively.
32 Ibid., p. 1008.
33 Ibid., pp. 1016; 1050; VII, pp. 17–20, 58–59, respectively.
34 Department of State, *Nazi-Soviet Relations, 1939–1941*, Documents from the Archives of the German Foreign Office, edited by James Sontag and James Stuart Beddie (Washington, D.C.: U.S. Government Printing Office, 1948), p. 77.
35 For Seeds's report dated July 24, see *DBFP*, 3rd Series, VI, pp. 456–60.
36 For the minutes of the fourth meeting of the Franco-British-Soviet military delegates, see *DBFP*, 3rd Series, VII, pp. 570–75.
37 For the full text of Seeds's memoranda dated August 15, 1939, see *DBFP*, 3rd Series, VII, pp. 1–5; also pp. 25–26, 39–40.
38 Bonnet, *Défense de la paix*, II, pp. 280–84; Leon Noël, *L'Aggression allemande contre la Pologne: Une ambassade à Varsovie, 1935–1939* (Paris: Flammarion, 1946), p. 423; *DBFP*, 3rd Series, VII, pp. 53–54.
39 For Bullitt's report, see *FRUS*, 1939, I, pp. 225–26.
40 See Assemblé Nationale, *Les événements*, IV, pp. 861–63 (Noël's testimony).
41 *DGFP*, Series D, VII, pp. 62–64, 84–85, 150–51, 156–57, 168, respectively.
42 *DBFP*, 3rd Series, VII, pp. 117, 130.
43 Ibid., p. 150; also Joseph Beck, *Dernier rapport: Politique polonaise, 1926–1939* (Neuchâtel: Editions de la Baconnière, 1951), pp. 202–4.
44 *DBFP*, 3rd Series, VII, pp. 609–13.
45 For the photostatic copies of the German and Russian texts of both the pact and the secret protocol, see Jean Comte Szembek, *Diariusz i Teki Jana Szembeka (Diary and Archives of Jan Szembek)*, 4 vols. (London: Polish Research Center, 1964–1972), IV, pp. 752–62.
46 *DGFP*, Series D, VII, p. 228. Some seven years later, Göring and Ribbentrop expressed the same views as defendants in the Nuremburg trial, see *The Trial of the Major War Criminals before the International Military Tribunal*, Nuremberg, 14 November 1945–1 October 1946, (Nuremberg:1947), 42 vols. IX, p. 345; X, 267–69; see also Joachim von Ribbentrop, *The Ribbentrop Memoirs* (London: Weidenfeld and Nicolson, 1954), pp. 111–12.
47 *PWB*, pp. 187–89.
48 Gustav Hilger and Alfred G. Meyer, *The Incompatible Allies, a Memoir-History of German-Soviet Relations, 1918–1941* (New York: Macmillan, 1953), pp. 300.

CHAPTER 5

Vietnam: Civil War or War of Aggression?

JOSEPH S. SEBES, S.J.

Among the many distinctions for which Father Sebes will be remembered was the required survey course he taught for those School of Foreign Service students who elected it in lieu of theology (and appreciatively dubbed it "Buddhism for Baptists"). Father Sebes was an expert in Chinese history and the sometime regent and dean of the School of Foreign Service (and of the School of Business Administration). His incisive essay on Vietnam was the cover article in the Winter 1966 issue of the *Georgetown Magazine*. Writing in 1965 on the nature of the war in Vietnam to that time, he weighed opposing views and considered the legal and moral complexities of sovereignty and nonintervention related to that war.

The editors of that Winter 1966 *Georgetown Magazine* embedded in the article a box revealing evidence of Father Sebes's prescience (although he had astutely anticipated by several months the Diem regime's November 1963 demise, at the time he wrote this piece Father Sebes could not yet have discovered, and thus did not note, the U.S. role in the coup that toppled Diem):

> In the past three years, Father Sebes, as a close student of affairs in the Far East, has made three predictions: (1) On CBS television on August 1963, at the height of the Buddhist revolt and self-immolation, he predicted that by January 1, 1964, either the Diem regime would be out of power or the United States would be out of Vietnam (this prediction came true on November 1, 1963). (2) During the 1964 presidential campaign he predicted that if Johnson were elected the United States would bomb North Vietnam within four months (this prediction came true in February 1965). (3) Several months ago [in 1965] he predicted that if after the end of the monsoon season, mid-November 1965, North Vietnam did not show willingness to negotiate, the United States would expand its bombardment of military targets to property targets, thus bringing North Vietnam to the conference table.

Vietnam: Civil War or War of Aggression?

A Divided American Public

Our involvement in the Vietnamese war and the decision of our government to carry the war to North Vietnam by bombing military targets in the Democratic Republic of Vietnam (DRV) north of the 17th parallel have split American public opinion down the middle. A presentation of the opposing points of view may serve to place the problem in focus.

The U.S. Government's Position. Secretary of Defense Robert McNamara, in his speech at the Forrestal Memorial Award Dinner on March 26, 1964, defined the objectives of the United States in South Vietnam as threefold:

> First, and most important, is the simple fact that South Vietnam, a member of the free world family, is striving to preserve its independence from Communist attack. The [South] Vietnamese have asked for our help. We have given it. We shall continue to give it. We do so in their interest; and we do so in our own clear self-interest. The ultimate goal of the U. S. in Southeast Asia, as in the rest of the world, is to maintain free and independent nations which can develop politically, economically, and socially, and which can be responsible members of the world community.
> Second, Southeast Asia has great strategic significance in the forward defense of the U.S. . . . In Communist hands, this area would pose a most serious threat to the security of the U. S. and to the family of free world nations to which we belong. To defend Southeast Asia, we must meet the challenge in South Vietnam.
> And third, South Vietnam is a test case for the new Communist Strategy. . . . In January 1961, Chairman Khrushchev

Joseph S. Sebes, S.J.

made one of the most important speeches [on Communist strategy] of recent decades, [stating]: "In modern conditions the following categories of wars should be distinguished: world wars, local wars, liberation wars, and popular uprisings." He ruled out what he called, "world wars" and "local wars" as being too dangerous for profitable indulgence in a world of nuclear weapons. But with regard to what he called "liberation war," he referred specifically to Vietnam. He said, "It is a sacred war. We recognize such wars."

Our global posture for deterrence and defense is good enough to make the first two types of wars costly for Communism. President Kennedy and President Johnson have recognized, however, that our forces for the first two types of wars might not be applicable or effective against what the Communists call "wars of liberation" or what is properly called covert aggression or insurgency. We have therefore undertaken and continue to press a variety of programs to develop skilled specialists, equipment, and techniques to enable us to help our allies counter the threat of insurgency.

The U. S. role in South Vietnam, then, is: first, to answer the call of the South Vietnamese, a member nation of our free-world family, to help them save their country for themselves; second, to help prevent the strategic danger which would exist if Communism absorbed Southeast Asia's people and resources; and third, to prove in the Vietnam test case that the free world can cope with Communist "wars of liberation" as we have coped successfully with Communist aggression at other levels.

This course of action was chosen from among several alternatives open to us, alternatives Mr. McNamara described in the following terms:

> Some critics of our present policy have suggested one option—that we simply withdraw. This the U. S. totally rejects. . . . Other critics have called for a second and similar option—a neutralization of Vietnam. [But] neutralization of South Vietnam, which is today under unprovoked subversive attack, would not be in any sense an achievement [because] no one seriously believes that the Communists would agree to the neutralization of North Vietnam. As . . . in Laos, we have no objection in principle to neutrality in the sense of

Vietnam: Civil War or War of Aggression?

> nonalignment. But . . . Communist abuse of the Geneva Accords, by treating the Laos corridor as a sanctuary for infiltration, constantly threatens the precarious neutrality. Neutralization of South Vietnam—an ambiguous phrase at best—was therefore rejected.
>
> The third option . . . was initiation of military actions outside South Vietnam, particularly against North Vietnam, in order to supplement the counterinsurgency program in South Vietnam. This course of action . . . has been carefully studied. Whatever ultimate course of action may be forced upon us by the other side, it is clear that actions under this option would be only a supplement to, not a substitute for, progress within South Vietnam's own borders.
>
> The fourth course of action [the one being followed at the time of Mr. McNamara's speech] was to concentrate on helping the South Vietnamese win the battle in their own country. This, all agree, is essential no matter what else is done.

Since that time the United States has adopted the third option and for the past ten months has bombed military targets in North Vietnam.

The Opposition View. One of the most articulate opponents of American policy in Vietnam is Hans J. Morgenthau. In the *New York Times Magazine* (April 18, 1965) he wrote:

> Until the end of last February [1965], the government of the United States started from the assumption that the war in South Vietnam was a civil war, aided and abetted but not created from abroad, and spokesmen for the government have made time and again the point that the key to winning the war was political and not military and was to be found in South Vietnam itself . . . in transforming the indifference or hostility of the great mass of the South Vietnamese people into positive loyalty to the government. To that end, a new theory of warfare called counter-insurgency was put into practice . . . but . . . the population remained indifferent, if not hostile. . . .
>
> The reasons for this failure are of general significance, for they stem from a deeply ingrained habit of the American mind. We like to think of social problems as technically self-

Joseph S. Sebes, S.J.

sufficient and susceptible of simple, clear-cut solutions. . . . Thus, our military theoreticians and practitioners conceive of counter-insurgency as though it were just another branch of warfare. . . . This view derives, of course, from a complete misconception of the nature of civil war. People fight and die in civil wars because they have a faith which appears to them worth fighting and dying for, and they can be opposed with a chance of success only by people who have at least as strong a faith. In South Vietnam there is nothing to oppose the faith of the Vietcong and, in consequence, the Saigon government and we are losing the civil war.

The United States has recognized that it is failing in South Vietnam. But it has drawn from this recognition of failure a most astounding conclusion. The United States has decided to change the character of the war by unilateral declaration from a South Vietnamese civil war to a war of "foreign aggression." *Aggression from the North: The Record of North Vietnam's Campaign to Conquer South Vietnam* is the title of a white paper published by the Department of State on the last day of February 1965. While normally foreign and military policy is based upon intelligence—that is, the objective assessment of fact—the process is here reversed: a new policy has been decided upon, and intelligence must provide the facts to justify it. The United States, stymied in South Vietnam and on the verge of defeat, decided to carry the war to North Vietnam not so much in order to retrieve the fortunes of war as to lay the groundwork for "negotiations from strength."

In order to justify that new policy, it was necessary to prove that North Vietnam is the real enemy. It is the white paper's purpose to present that proof. Let it be said right away that the white paper is a dismal failure. The discrepancy between its assertions and the factual evidence adduced to support them borders on the grotesque. It does nothing to disprove, and tends even to confirm, what until the end of February had been official American doctrine: that the main body of the Vietcong is composed of South Vietnamese and that 80 per cent to 90 per cent of their weapons are of American origin. This document is most disturbing in that it provides a particularly glaring instance of the tendency to conduct foreign and military policy not on their own merits, but as exercises in public relations. The government fash-

Vietnam: Civil War or War of Aggression?

ions an imaginary world that pleases it, and then comes to believe in the reality of that world and acts as though it were real.

Here, then, are the two opposing views, in the words of outstanding spokesmen, of the issue at the heart of the American presence in Vietnam: Is the war in South Vietnam a "civil war," or is it a "war of aggression"? That there should be disagreement on this relatively simple question is an indication of the underlying complexity of the situation. An objective presentation of the problem—and especially of the key role of the Geneva Conference of 1954 in shaping its present dimensions—should enable us to see the entire tragic confrontation with greater clarity.

THE GENEVA AGREEMENTS OF 1954

Since it is primarily Vietnamese who are fighting Vietnamese, we may say that from an ethnic point of view the war is a civil war, "a war between different sections or parties of the same country and nation." But this is not all it is. For a full understanding of the nature of the war we must take a look at the Geneva Conference of 1954.

After the cease-fire agreement in Korea, in July 1953, Chinese Communist equipment, troops, and logistic help were given in increased quantities to the Viet Minh forces, who had been fighting the French in Indochina since December 1946. At home the French government was under increasing pressure to negotiate a settlement along the lines of the Korean settlement. At a meeting of President Eisenhower, Prime Minister Churchill, and Prime Minister Joseph Laniel in Bermuda in December 1953, it was decided that both the Korean and Indochinese questions should be discussed with the Soviet Union at the foreign minister level.

This meeting of foreign ministers took place in Berlin in 1954; and here it was agreed to call a conference of interested powers to be held at Geneva in April to discuss both the Korean and Indochinese questions. In order to be able to negotiate from strength at Geneva, the Viet Minh forces greatly

JOSEPH S. SEBES, S.J.

intensified their attacks against the French. Thus by the time the conference began at Geneva on April 27, 1954, the fall of Dienbienphu seemed inevitable, and the Indochinese question completely overshadowed the soon-stalemated negotiations concerning Korea. By May 8, when the delegates turned their attention to Indochina, Dienbienphu had already fallen. Before their final collapse, the French felt that the only way to prevent a military disaster would be through open American intervention.

An American Military Advisory Group had been with French forces since July 1950. American aid had totaled close to a billion dollars by the time the fighting ended. Contingents of the Seventh Fleet, with Marines combat-ready and airplanes to give air support, were standing by. Yet it was decided not to intervene. It was too soon after Korea to become involved in another Asian conflict, especially in support of a colonial power.

Because of its importance and repercussions on world peace the Geneva Conference was attended not only by the belligerents, France and the Viet Minh, but also by Great Britain, the Soviet Union, and the United States, the Indochinese member states of the French Union (Vietnam, Cambodia, and Laos), and, finally, the People's Republic of China. The agreements reached at Geneva may be grouped under two headings: the cease-fire agreement between the French and the Viet Minh high commands concerning Vietnam, Cambodia, and Laos, and the Final Declaration of Intent.[1] Let us examine them one by one.

The Cease-Fire Agreement. The cease-fire agreement, although negotiated by politicians on the highest diplomatic level, was signed by the military authorities on both sides: General Henri Delteil, representing the French High Command in Indochina, and General Ta Quang Buu for the Viet Minh. This cease-fire agreement was signed on July 20, when the previously reluctant Molotov ordered the Viet Minh to accept the 17th parallel as the dividing line. According to P. J. Honey, "Mr. Molotov would appear to have exploited the situation to Russia's advantage by concluding a secret agreement with M. Mendès-France

Vietnam: Civil War or War of Aggression?

whereby the Communists would accord France generous armistice terms in Indochina in return for France's rejection of the European Defense Community. Pham Van Dong was then ordered to sign the agreements, regardless of the DRV loss of face, and he meekly complied."[2]

The Saigon delegation also opposed the signing of the ceasefire agreement, and its foreign minister protested "against the hasty conclusion of an armistice by the French High Command alone."[3] The Saigon delegation insisted on the territorial unity of Vietnam and elections under UN supervision in all Vietnam. The Western powers, however, feeling that partition would be unavoidable, rendered Saigon's opposition void. The document signed by the two generals is officially known as the "Agreement on the Cessation of Hostilities in Viet-Nam, July 20, 1954."

The two zones into which Vietnam was divided were called "temporary regroupment areas." Chapter I of the agreement establishes a demarcation line and a demilitarized zone along the 17th parallel. Chapter II deals with the moving of troops and equipment through one another's zones. For instance, Article 14, under the heading "Political and administrative measures in the two regrouping zones, on either side of the provisional military demarcation line," states:

> (a) Pending general elections which will bring about the unification of Vietnam, the conduct of civil administration in each regrouping zone shall be in the hands of the party whose forces are to be regrouped there.... (b) Any territory controlled by one party which is transferred to the other party by the regrouping plan shall continue to be administered by the former party until such date as all the troops who are to be transferred have completely left.... The transfer shall be effected in successive stages for the various territorial sectors.... (c) Each party undertakes to refrain from any reprisals or discrimination against persons or organizations on account of their activities during the hostilities and to guarantee their democratic liberties. (d) From the date of entry into force of the present Agreement until the movement of troops is completed, any civilians residing in a district controlled by one party who wish to go and live in the

zone assigned to the other party shall be permitted and helped to do so by the authorities in that district.

Chapter III is entitled "Ban on the Introduction of Fresh Troops, Military Personnel, Arms, and Munitions. Military Bases." Chapter IV considers "Prisoners of War and Civilian Internees." Chapter V is entitled "Miscellaneous." Article 24 of this chapter is of special importance. It reads: "The present Agreement shall apply to all the armed forces of either side. The armed forces of each party shall respect the demilitarized zone and the territory under the military control of the other party, and shall commit no act and undertake no operation against the other party. . . ."

Chapter VI establishes the International Commission for Supervision and Control (popularly known as the International Control Commission, or ICC), composed of neutral Indian (presiding), pro-Western Canadian, and Communist Polish members to supervise the execution of the cease-fire provisions with the help of fixed and mobile teams. This chapter also provides for a system of joint commissions, consisting of representatives of the two opposing armies and operating in teams in order to ensure the execution of the simultaneous cease-fire for all regular and irregular armed forces, the regroupment of these armed forces, and observance of the demarcation line. These are the major provisions of the cease-fire agreement for Vietnam.

The Final Declaration. The "Final Declaration of the Geneva Conference on the Problem of Restoring Peace in Indo-China, July 21, 1954" was necessary because the cease-fire agreements had left the political arrangements (for Vietnam) unresolved. These were settled on July 21, at a final meeting at which Anthony Eden presided. Eden read off a list of documents that were part of the record and that became known as the Final Declaration.

Some of the declaration's more important provisions are contained in Articles 6 and 7, which state that the military demarcation line was to be provisional and not to be considered as a

Vietnam: Civil War or War of Aggression?

political or territorial boundary. It was further provided that the settlement of political problems "effected on the basis of respect for the principles of independence and territorial integrity shall permit the Vietnamese people to enjoy fundamental freedoms, guaranteed by democratic institutions established as a result of free general elections by secret ballot." Article 7 further states that "general elections shall be held in July 1956, under the supervision of an international commission composed of the Member States of the International Supervisory Commission."

The spokesman of every participating delegation gave his oral approval to the declaration with the exception of the American and the Saigon delegations. The disagreement of these two delegations was described by Bernard B. Fall: "Then it was the turn of Under Secretary of State Walter Bedell Smith of the United States," who said his government was not prepared to join in such a declaration by the conference. "Instead, he submitted a separate declaration in which the United States affirmed that it would 'refrain from the threat or the use of force to disturb' the agreements but would view 'any renewal of the aggression in violation of the aforesaid agreements with grave concern and as seriously threatening international peace and security,' [adding] that in the 'case of nations divided against their will,' the United States supported efforts 'to achieve unity through free elections supervised by the United Nations.'"[4]

Fall placed the American role in Geneva in context. "Under pressure from home not to give the impression of 'approving a surrender to Communism,'" the U.S. delegation "had for all practical purposes ceased to influence events. Secretary Dulles had left Geneva on May 4, even before the Indochina conference began.[5] In President Eisenhower's words, the 'American delegation [was] downgraded to an "observer" mission.' This attempt at saving face at home was to have important consequences as the negotiations reached their climax."[6]

It is interesting to note how the pressure of public opinion has changed in eleven years. Today [in 1965] a segment of American opinion wants us to get out of Vietnam and surrender South Vietnam to Communism.

Joseph S. Sebes, S.J.

The other dissenting voice to the acceptance of the declaration was that of Dr. Tran Van Do, the foreign minister of the Ngo Dinh Diem cabinet that had been established by Emperor Bao Dai, puppet chief of state of Vietnam under the French, on June 16, 1954. "Cold-shouldered by everyone, Dr. Do had fought a lonely battle," according to Fall, "trying to save his country from partition and what then seemed imminent domination by Ho Chi Minh." Dr. Do made his "final plea, but the matter was obviously considered settled by everyone else. All that he could obtain was that the other conferees 'take note' of [South] Vietnam's promise 'not to use force to resist the procedures for carrying the cease-fire into effect.'"[7]

Thus, the Final Declaration was accepted by the majority but it was not signed by anyone; it remained an *unsigned document*. "This fact," as Fall pointed out, had "not entirely escaped astute observers, and surely was not an oversight on the part of the negotiators in either camp.... This absence of signature, [according to observers], 'would permit [the participants] to act as if the organization of elections in Vietnam within two years had been a simple project' rather than a formal commitment, [and] 'the Geneva Conference will thus have invited a new form of peaceful coexistence—that which results from the tacit consent of the negotiators—as well as a new form of legal obligation between states: the unsigned treaty.'"[8]

Geneva's Aftermath. Under the terms of the Geneva Agreements, the independence of Vietnam was stated in unequivocal terms (Articles 10, 11, and 12 of the Final Declaration), but it was a divided country. The agreements had stipulated the regrouping of military forces and the free movement of civilians. Accordingly, close to 100,000 (Viet Minh regulars, guerrillas, civilians, and their dependents) moved from south to north of the 17th parallel. Thousands of local guerrillas, many of them elite communist cadres, remained, hid their arms, and became, for the time being, simple villagers.

Meanwhile, close to 200,000 Franco-Vietnamese troops moved south of the demarcation line. In addition, close to a million civilians fled southward. A much greater number at-

Vietnam: Civil War or War of Aggression?

tempted to leave but were prevented by the Viet Minh, who took over the country as the French were leaving. Since then, over 200,000 more have reached sanctuary in the south by escaping in small boats and bamboo rafts. It will never be known how many refugees perished at sea or were captured.

For the Viet Minh the Geneva Agreements were far from satisfactory. Acceptance of the 17th parallel as the dividing line meant relinquishing territory they held in the south. Eight years of war had won the Communists only the northern half of Vietnam, a food deficit area that was in ruins. The frontier between the two halves would be policed by the ICC, a fact that would make penetration of the south across the 17th parallel difficult.

Viet Minh failure to secure control of the whole of Vietnam involved no small loss of face, since they had always promised to continue the war until the entire country was "liberated." Yet, in spite of all this the Viet Minh agreed. They did so because they were given no alternative. They were forced to do so by the two major Communist powers, Russia and China, then still working in harmony.

Faced with the possibility of direct American intervention, Russia and China decided that the risk of not reaching an agreement was too great. To offset the drawbacks involved in the agreements, there were also some advantages for the Viet Minh. French defeat had given them tremendous prestige. If they had to accept the presence of the ICC, at least one member, Poland, was favorably disposed, and India made no secret of her sympathy for North rather than South Vietnam. It would therefore be simple in practice to circumvent the ICC and prevent its teams from visiting places that might prove embarrassing. Moreover, the situation in the south was full of promise, since South Vietnam was in chaos.

Civil War or Aggression?

Having examined the Geneva Accords of 1954, we can say that while the conferees did not intend to establish, *de jure* and permanently, two separate countries or political entities, *de facto* two separate countries came into existence and have existed

Joseph S. Sebes, S.J.

ever since. Nor can the blame for this *de facto* situation be laid exclusively at the doorsteps of South Vietnam and the United States. Both of these nations refused to agree even to the temporary partition of Vietnam, realizing that elections after two years of Communist control in the north could neither be free nor meaningful.

DRV agitation for elections began only after Communist hopes for taking over South Vietnam without a fight had been foiled by a strong Diem regime. (In 1954, nobody gave the Diem regime a chance of surviving more than six months.) At the end of the Geneva Conference, Pham Van Dong, head of the Viet Minh delegation (later prime minister of the DRV), when questioned as to who would win the elections in 1956, answered, "You know as well as I do that there aren't going to be any elections."[9]

Even when the DRV started to agitate for elections, neither Russia nor China gave its wholehearted support on this issue of elections. In early 1957, the Soviet Union proposed the admission of both Vietnams to the United Nations, thus expressing the belief that there were *de facto* two Vietnams. It should be remembered that at that time Russia and China were still in close collaboration, thus the Russian view reflects the view of the Communist bloc.

Nor is a divided Vietnam or the existence of two Vietnams a unique phenomenon on the world scene today. We find two Chinas, two Germanys, and two Koreas. Thus there are precedents. But even with regard to Vietnam itself, there is historical precedent for a division of Vietnam roughly along the North-South dividing lines. Such a division lasted from 1674 to 1802, when Vietnam was unified and the Nguyen dynasty began. Vietnam remained a unified country for only fifty-six years, however. The French divided the country once again, this time into three parts: Tonkin, Annam, and Cochin China. This division, too, had its precedent in earlier history.

Civil War? No. Granting the *de facto* existence of two Vietnams, does not the fact that a great number of the Vietcong are South Vietnamese prove that the war is a civil war? And do not, it

Vietnam: Civil War or War of Aggression?

might be argued, the existence of the National Front for the Liberation of South Vietnam (NFLSV) and the South Vietnamese People's Revolutionary Party (SVPRP), both founded in 1961, confirm the fact that a civil war exists?

Whatever plausibility such arguments might possess falls before the stubborn fact that the subversion of the Vietcong started as a deliberate DRV policy of leaving subversive agents behind in South Vietnam after the division of the country. Many of the Vietcong therefore are hard-core Communist cadres of the Communist party of North Vietnam. Many other South Vietnamese have been terrorized into joining the Vietcong. Further, the NFLSV and the SVPRP were organized, directed, and used for the purpose of complementing North Vietnam's military efforts by means of, respectively, a political offensive in the form of an all-party united front and a new Marxist-Leninist party to infiltrate and manipulate that united front.

Thus it would seem eminently reasonable to conclude that the war in Vietnam is, at the very least, a war of covert aggression by the DRV against South Vietnam. In recent months the presence of entire DRV regular battalions, and even divisions, has been definitively established.

Is Intervention Justified?

In view of all this it would seem that the war in Vietnam is a war of aggression by the DRV against South Vietnam, and the DRV, not South Vietnam and the United States, has violated the Geneva Accords. But are we violating international law by having intervened in Vietnam, as some antagonists of our government's policy state? International law defines intervention as "the interference of a state in the affairs of another state for the purpose of compelling it to do or forbear certain acts or to maintain or alter an internal condition." Under the UN Charter and the Charter of the Organization of American States, the United States has committed itself to seemingly inflexible principles of nonintervention in the internal affairs of other states. Yet, this country has intervened in a number of cases. There seems to be, therefore, a serious gap between our legal commitments and our conduct.

Joseph S. Sebes, S.J.

But is intervention legally wrong? The majority view among prevailing normative theories holds that while intervention is wrong *prima facie*, exceptions to the general rule are permitted. Nonetheless, there is a heavy burden of proof upon the party invoking such an exception, the presumption always being against intervention.

Underlying the principle of nonintervention are (1) the principle of state sovereignty and of sovereign equality of states; and (2) the right of nations to self-determination. Both of these principles seem to assume that the protection of sovereignty and of the right of self-determination are more important than any other values so far as the problem of intervention is concerned. Exceptions to the principle of nonintervention have included the following as justifications: (1) self-defense, (2) counterintervention, (3) preemptive intervention, (4) protection of nationals' lives and property, (5) humanitarian intervention, (6) antitotalitarian intervention, and (7) intervention by invitation. Let us now see how the United States has justified its intervention in South Vietnam.

The primary justification is counterintervention by invitation. I prefer to lump counterintervention and intervention by invitation together because, in my opinion, the two together add up to a better justification than they would furnish separately. If the state is endowed with sovereignty, and if nations or peoples have the right to constitute themselves into independent sovereign states by an act of self-determination, then it follows that states must have the right to defend their sovereignty and to invite others to help them do so.

The foreign minister of South Vietnam, Vu Van Mau, in November 1961, pointed precisely to this principle of international law in order to justify to the ICC (which had just submitted its report) United States intervention by invitation in his country. The ICC seems to have accepted this explanation because its report does cite the South Vietnamese explanation that whatever U.S. help it was receiving was for the purpose of fighting DRV subversion.

Vietnam: Civil War or War of Aggression?

But who has the right to "invite"? The answer evidently must be: the legitimately established representative government of a sovereign state. But did the Diem government, in 1961, possess these attributes? In my opinion it did. And may the right to "invite" be altered by changes in the relationship between the South Vietnamese people and the government in power? The answer evidently must be: Yes, if the South Vietnamese people should decide that they do not want their government to exercise this right.

None of the nine governments in power since 1961 nor the Vietnamese people have expressed their desire to terminate or revoke their invitation. Quite the contrary is true. Popular discontent has overthrown several governments but never in order to revoke its "invitation." Whether or not the right to intervene by invitation ceases at the point at which the rebels have in fact taken over substantial control of the country is a moot question; they have not yet done so. Not only have they not succeeded in doing so in South Vietnam, but they have not even done so in Laos, where they control a much larger part of the country.

Another question arises: What kind and degree of intervention agreed to or condoned by the South Vietnamese government is permissible? Since United States intervention by invitation is counterintervention, we must first study the justification for counterintervention before answering the question. If there is a legal-ethical right to collective self-defense against direct armed aggression, there must be a derivative right to come to the aid of a victim of such indirect aggression as civil conflict organized, directed, and supplied by an outside aggressor. Vietcong action in South Vietnam is this at the very least.

Consequently the nature, degree, and form of United States intervention, since it is counterintervention, must be decided by the nature, degree, and form of the aggression that provoked it. To be more specific, many experts in international law hold that the existence of a clear and present threat to the state's vital interests or national existence arising out of conditions within another state—such as the mounting of a serious military

Joseph S. Sebes, S.J.

threat, or encouragement or tolerance of continuous subversive and terrorist activity—might give rise to a right of intervention in self-defense.

Thus, Vietcong action organized, directed, and supplied by North Vietnam, presents a clear and present threat to the vital interests and national existence of South Vietnam and thereby gives South Vietnam the right, in self-defense, of intervention in North Vietnam. And it also gives the United States, by invitation, the right to aid South Vietnam in this intervention in its self-defense. If intervention is at all justifiable, then we can conclude that United States counterintervention by invitation is, up to this point, well within the limits of international law.

Vietnam: Civil War or War of Aggression?

Endnotes

1. For the Geneva Agreements, see *American Policy 1950–1955, Basic Documents*, Volume I, Part 3, I–IX, Department of State Publications 6446, General Foreign Policy Series 117, p. 750. For further details, see also P. J. Honey in several numbers of *China News Analysis*, and Bernard B. Fall, "That Geneva Agreement-How the French Got Out of Vietnam," *New York Times Magazine*, May 2, 1965, pp. 28, 113–17, and 119.
2. P. J. Honey, in *China News Analysis*, No. 389, p.3.
3. Ibid., p. 2.
4. Fall, "That Geneva Agreement," p. 114.
5. It was on May 8, after the negotiations concerning Korea had reached a stalemate, that the delegates took up the issue of Indochina.
6. Fall, "That Geneva Agreement," p. 113.
7. Ibid., p. 114.
8. Ibid., p. 115.
9. Honey, in *China News Analysis*, No. 389, p. 2.

CHAPTER 6

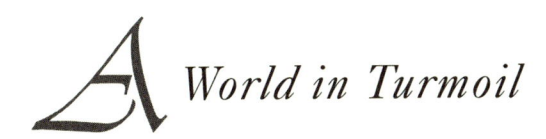

A World in Turmoil

JULES DAVIDS

Jules Davids taught U.S. diplomatic history at Georgetown from 1946 to 1986, a period of prodigious additions to that history. In his preface to the third edition of his *America and the World of Our Time: U.S. Diplomacy in the Twentieth Century* (Random House, 1970), he noted the "veritable transformation of American life and explosive developments in many parts of the world" that had occurred just in the eight years since the book's second edition. The many School of Foreign Service students who studied with Professor Davids will recognize his voice in these excerpts from that book's final chapter, which began with an epigraph from biologist George Wald declaring, "Our challenge is to give what account we can of what becomes . . . of all [people] of all nations, colors, and creeds."

A World in Turmoil

Many of the assumptions that guided America's actions in the past have been shaken by changes both within the United States and in the world order. The weapons, technological, and space revolutions in the nuclear age, among other things, have ended America's continental security, altered the economic structures of societies, changed the determinants of power, and stimulated reevaluations of the role of sovereignty and the functions of the political state.

At the end of World War II, it was impossible to foresee the impact of the nuclear age. The pursuit of security was largely viewed in terms of the preatomic World War II period. Thus, a major concern of the Allied wartime leaders was in establishing an organization that would be capable of dealing with aggression and in creating a more effective international institution than the League of Nations to ensure peaceful change in the world order.

The United Nations was intended as an instrument for this purpose, but reliance was also placed on the continued cooperation of the victorious Allied powers. When the Cold War ensued instead, the United States looked beyond the United Nations. For purposes of security, it concentrated on building up "situations of strength" both by increasing its own military power and by forging collective defense systems. These measures were supplemented by efforts to improve the economic conditions of other countries to eliminate the sources of discontent that were believed to nourish communism.

The Soviet Union responded to these actions by acquiring its own nuclear capability, by consolidating its control over Eastern Europe, and by attempting to weaken and ultimately destroy the NATO alliance and thus remove the American military presence in Europe. As the United States and the Soviet Union

Jules Davids

built up their nuclear arsenals and through technological improvements increased the destructiveness of these weapons, a "balance of nuclear terror" was attained that diminished the likelihood of a global nuclear war. Fear nevertheless persisted that this balance could be decisively altered as a result of a technological "breakthrough." The nuclear arms race thus continued.

The search for peace related not only to steps adopted by the two superpowers to ensure their own physical security, but to their efforts to cultivate an environment that would be conducive to their own interests. Neither Washington nor Moscow, however, foresaw the explosive situation that would develop as a consequence of decolonization.

After World War II, the rise of national revolutions in Asia, the Middle East, and Africa hastened the dismantling of the European colonial systems, and in varying degrees shattered traditional societies. Largely inspired by the twofold objectives of attaining political independence and economic betterment, this movement was directed against the eradication of Western rule and Western influence, as well as toward adjusting native societies to meet the pressures of the modern world.

But the national revolutions in emerging new nations also awakened regional rivalries, and heightened cultural, racial, religious, and psychological tensions. Since these regions contained the vast majority of the world's population and possessed the raw materials upon which the West was greatly dependent, they inevitably became involved in the Cold War.

Although the climate of the 1960s was shaped by many things, events and developments in four areas—Africa, Southeast Asia (especially Vietnam), the Middle East, and arms control—were of crucial significance. *[Excerpted here are the chapter's sections on Africa and arms control. —Ed.]*

Under Africa's Volcano

Among all the regions in the world, Africa was the one the United States was perhaps least prepared to deal with. Before World War II, American contacts with that continent had been slight. To be sure, Yankee traders, at an early date, were famil-

A World in Turmoil

iar with its coastline and ports and engaged in the profitable slave trade. The United States had also been involved in continuing quarrels with the rulers of the Barbary Coast, which were not ended until 1816. Six years later, it helped establish Liberia as an independent state.

In 1884–1885, American delegates participated in the Berlin Conference that marked the formal partition of Africa into colonial spheres and recognized the Belgian king Leopold's "Congo Free State." American missionaries and educators had continued their activities in Africa. Although the United States tried to keep the Congo region and Europe's colonies open to American trade and missionary activities, it looked upon Africa, particularly after the Berlin Conference, as an area primarily of European responsibility. Until the 1960s, Washington strictly avoided any direct involvement in African affairs.

Only four countries in the whole of Africa—Ethiopia, Liberia, Egypt, and South Africa—retained in their several ways a nominal independence in 1945; the rest of the continent remained a European imperial preserve. During the next two decades, this situation dramatically changed, with an almost fourfold increase in the number of newly created independent states. In 1960 alone, the so-called "Year of Africa," the United Nations admitted sixteen new African states. Though the Sudan, Morocco, and Tunisia had secured complete independence in 1956, and Egypt had asserted its independence in the Suez War, the event marking a decisive "breakthrough" had come in 1957, when Britain ended its colonial rule in the "Gold Coast" and Ghana became the first "black" state to be granted independence.

Since 1945, three key issues have largely dominated African affairs: the struggle to acquire political freedom; the movement to create Pan-African unity; and the efforts to eliminate colonialism and white man's rule wherever it still existed. The rapid demise of European colonialism was the result of a combination of circumstances. Among some of the contributing factors were the effects of World War II, which seriously weakened the European imperial powers politically and economically; the determination of African nationalist leaders to attain political equality and to end the discrimination that had kept them out of the seats of power; the changed intellectual climate in Europe that increasingly brought into question the virtues of imperialistic policies; the anticolonial propaganda of the Soviet Union and Communist China; America's avowal of the principle of self-determination; and the impact of the "revolution of rising expectations," which made many Africans, especially those who had been abroad, unwilling to accept previous conditions.

More immediately, the revolutionary upheavals in Indochina and Algeria, together with the Anglo-French setback in the Suez incident, acted as catalysts in stimulating Africa's independence movement. After Suez, France was shaken by a major domestic crisis. The threat of civil war in 1958 by a million-odd French settlers in Algeria, backed by powerful elements in the French armed forces, toppled the Fourth Republic and brought General Charles De Gaulle to power. De Gaulle, however, instead of supporting the continuation of French control, took steps to extend independence to Algeria, much to the frustration of his original backers. Peace talks, initiated in 1960, finally led to the signing of a series of political accords at Evian-les-Bains in March 1962 that resulted in a cease-fire and the prompt ending of the seven-year Algerian war. Four months later, on July 3, France acknowledged the full independence of the Algerian Republic.

The Congo Erupts. Though the struggles in Indochina and Algeria had significant repercussions, the event that brought Africa to the center of the world stage was the Congo crisis of 1960–61. The chaotic upheaval in the Congo not only severely tested the prestige of the United Nations, but compelled the United States to play a more active role in African affairs, disrupted the movement toward Pan-African unity, and stiffened the resistance of white-controlled countries in southern Africa—especially South Africa, Portuguese Angola and Mozambique, and Southern Rhodesia—against the possibility of black rule.

On June 30, 1960, Belgium granted independence to the Congo. Unprepared for self-government, the new state plummeted into disorder and violence. In the mistaken belief that

A World in Turmoil

by so doing they could perpetuate colonial rule, the Belgians had deliberately denied the Congolese the training and experience that would have enabled them to administer their own country. Although this situation existed in varying degrees in other European colonies, it proved to be particularly disastrous in the Congo.

During the next five years, the Congo was torn by continual strife. The problems centered on intense personal rivalries, intertribal warfare, dissension over the type of political system that should prevail, and conflicting attitudes over future relations with Belgium.

. . . .

The situation posed an acute dilemma in the United Nations. At the opening of the United Nations session in New York in September 1960, the question was raised as to which of two rival Congolese delegations should be seated [that of President Joseph Kasavubu or that of Prime Minister Patrice Lumumba, whom Kasavubu had dismissed]. That General Assembly meeting was the largest gathering of heads of state and government in the history of the international organization, and included the leaders of some dozen new African states. It quickly became apparent that the seating of the Congolese delegation went beyond the Congo crisis. There emerged a struggle for control over the United Nations itself.

Premier Khrushchev, who headed the Soviet delegation, launched a frontal attack against the structure of the Secretariat so that the United Nations could not be used to thwart Russia's interests. Denouncing the U.N.'s handling of the situation in the Congo—its refusal to support Lumumba in his efforts to crush the secessionist movements in Katanga and South Kasai—Khrushchev demanded that Dag Hammarsjöld resign and that the structure of the Secretariat be changed. Khrushchev declared that the organization of the United Nations no longer reflected the new balance of forces in the world. To remedy the situation, he urged that a triumvirate composed of one Western, one Communist, and one neutralist representative replace the Secretariat.

Jules Davids

The Soviet plan—the establishment of a so-called *troika*—would have meant that Russia could exert more control over the functions that had been conferred upon the secretary-general. During the debate on his proposals, Khrushchev, with calculated bad behavior—at one point he took off one of his shoes and used it to pound on the desk in front of him—deliberately tried to obstruct the Assembly's procedures. These maneuvers failed. As a result of the opposition that developed both within the United Nations and from the United States, the *troika* proposal and the attempt to prevent the seating of the Kasavubu delegation were rebuffed.

. . . .

The Search for Stability

The task of establishing stability both within the Congo and in other African states proved to be inordinately difficult. Four factors, in particular, hampered the attainment of this goal. First, tribal cultures and traditional patterns made it almost impossible to create any national cohesion and political unity; second, most African states had a conspicuous lack of indigenous capital and of technical, managerial, and administrative know-how; third, the exodus of Western Europeans—both voluntary and involuntary—who had a practical monopoly of these requisites for progress aggravated the problem of instability; finally, the European powers in the nineteenth century had carved out their colonies with little regard for ethnic or geographic considerations.

Geography posed an especially acute dilemma. Land routes from one country to another remained extremely primitive. Whatever railroads had been built ran only to the sea; Africa's commercial patterns, formed in the nineteenth century, were largely designed to suit the purposes of European colonial powers. Few of the African states after 1957 had viable economies; none was wholly self-sustaining, and some were all but helpless economically. Ethiopia and Sudan, with favorable climates and large areas of fertile land, were better off than most, but other African nations were fortunate if they had one or two raw materials or crops to exchange for the necessities of life.

A World in Turmoil

During the 1960s, the African continent found itself pulled in two directions: on the one hand, to develop regional groupings; and on the other, to safeguard the territorial sovereignty of individual states. Border clashes inevitably erupted as attempts were made to reclaim areas that contained inhabitants of similar ethnic origins. Although fundamentally preoccupied with colonial and related issues, as well as with internal struggles for power, the new African states were also anxious to strengthen their political and economic solidarity as a means of furthering their development and enlarging their influence in world affairs.

A clear-cut division between two groups of African states quickly became manifest on how to deal with African problems. The first group, composed of the so-called Casablanca countries—Ghana, the United Arab Republic [of Egypt and Syria], Morocco, Guinea, Mali, and Algeria—called for a militant Pan-African program urging the speedy creation of a union of African states with a central legislature, an attack against all vestiges of colonialism, and an attitude of "positive neutrality" in the Cold War. The second faction, identified with the "Monrovia group," included twelve French-speaking African states of the African-Malagasy Union, plus Ethiopia, Liberia, Somalia, the Republic of the Congo, and the British Commonwealth states of Nigeria and Sierra Leone.

Usually led by Nigeria and supported by Emperor Haile Selassie, the Monrovia powers favored a pragmatic and gradualist approach toward some form of association of African states, based on a confederation, rather than a unitary, or federal, arrangement. They held that practical cooperation in economic, technical, and cultural matters had to take precedence over African political unification, because, as Haile Selassie declared, "Tradition cannot be abandoned at once."

Despite the differences between the Casablanca and Monrovia groups, African leaders were determined to build a common front. Though they were at odds on how to effect a closer political union, they agreed that it was necessary to deal with the Congo crisis; to destroy the *apartheid* system in South Africa, which enforced the separation of the white and black

Jules Davids

races; to remove Portuguese colonialism from Angola and Mozambique; and to end white rule in Southern Rhodesia. In May 1963, leaders of over thirty African states assembled at Addis Ababa and agreed to set up an Organization of African Unity, which would meet annually. The OAU was to be entrusted with the task of settling all inter-African disputes and insulating the continent from external interference. It was, however, a grouping of wholly independent and sovereign states, and as such was similar in its structure to the Organization of American States in the Western Hemisphere.

A major test of the ability of the OAU to cope with the problems in Africa was posed by the continuing threats of disintegration in the Republic of the Congo (Leopoldville).... The Congo crises produced far-ranging repercussions. The prestige of the Organization of African Unity was badly damaged by its inability to exert an influence in establishing peace; the split between moderate and revolutionary African states widened; and resistance against the African nationalist movement intensified in South Africa, Rhodesia, and the Portuguese colonies. Dominant white groups in these regions steadfastly refused to accommodate themselves to African demands. Although the United Nations adopted countless resolutions demanding an end to South Africa's *apartheid* system, they continued to be rebuffed.

Nor was the United Nations [in those years] successful in dealing with the problem of South West Africa [which eventually became independent Namibia, with U.N. help—*Ed.*]. This ex-German colony had been administered by South Africa as a League of Nations mandate from 1920 to 1945. After World War II, however, it rejected any accountability to the United Nations and ruled the territory essentially on its own responsibility. Efforts of African states to reassert U.N. authority were seriously frustrated in 1966 when the World Court declined to hand down a formal ruling on the issue.

During the 1960s, African leaders strongly believed that drastic sanctions and coercion were necessary to end *apartheid* and to solve the South West Africa problem. But neither the United

A World in Turmoil

States nor Britain were willing to lend full support to such extreme proposals. Both countries had many companies and sizable investments in South Africa; the region was a source of strategic minerals, especially industrial diamonds; and it was the site of valuable American naval and space-tracking facilities. Though the United States repeatedly expressed its sympathy for African aspirations and proclaimed its devotion to the principle of self-determination, it was also clear that American officials opposed rash actions, not only because they jeopardized the nation's interests, but, more important, because they feared they would precipitate an explosion of racial violence of devastating proportions. Black Africans, however, viewed Washington's insistence on policies of restraint and moderation as simply a sanction for *apartheid* and white man's rule; they deeply resented America's vacillation and diffidence in condemning South Africa in the United Nations.

In Southern Rhodesia, where the white population of some 200,000 exercised political power over a 3.7 million African majority, steps were taken in November 1965 that further exacerbated racial tensions. Prime Minister Ian Douglas Smith, a white extremist who strongly supported a scheme for "community development" not greatly different from South Africa's policy of *apartheid*, unilaterally proclaimed Southern Rhodesia's independence. This act disregarded London's demand that the whites grant a greater degree of representation to Africans based on the principle of "one man, one vote," and the British viewed it as political rebellion.

London promptly imposed severe economic reprisals. The U.N Security Council, at the same time, unanimously condemned the unilateral declaration of independence, urged all states to deny recognition and aid to Rhodesia's "illegal racist minority regime," and called for an embargo on shipments of oil and petroleum products. But these measures failed to topple the rebel government. South Africa largely nullified the economic pressures by supplying Rhodesia with substantial quantities of boycotted items under the pretext of maintaining "normal trade." Attempts by African states in the United

JULES DAVIDS

Nations to close the South African loophole were unsuccessful; nor were they able to exert a decisive influence on the situation within the continent.

At the end of the 1960s, Africa's struggle for stability continued. In the south, the "battle line" between the white-ruled regions and black Africa became more firmly fixed. The grisly prospect of racial warfare in South Africa remained an ominous possibility. Guerrilla operations persisted in the Portuguese colonies, though on a lesser scale than had been the case earlier in the decade. Determined to hold on to its African territories, Portugal retained the bulk of its army of over 100,000 troops in Angola, Mozambique, and Portuguese Guinea. African nationalists made the ending of colonial rule in these areas an item of top priority.

In the meantime, political, economic, and tribal crises wracked many African states, resulting in numerous coups, countercoups, and assassinations. Late in 1965, Premier Moise Tshombe was deposed in the Congo. During the next year, major upheavals occurred in Nigeria and Ghana. The situation in Nigeria was especially alarming to the United States. The most populous and one of the richest of African countries, it had long been regarded by Washington as a showcase of stability on the continent. A military coup in January 1966 triggered tribal conflicts, particularly between the Ibos of eastern Nigeria and the Hausas of the north, who had exercised a dominant influence in the central government. Then, on February 24, a military coup took place in Ghana that led to the ouster of President Kwame Nkrumah while he was visiting the People's Republic of China.

The abrupt dislodgement of Nkrumah's regime marked a setback to the African revolutionary nationalist movement and widened the gulf between "radical" and "moderate" African states. After the failure of other African governments to effect conciliation, the Eastern Region of Nigeria carried out its threat to secede. On May 30, 1967, it declared itself an independent republic, taking the name of Biafra. The ensuing civil war lasted for thirty months. Biafra finally capitulated in January 1970, but domestic tensions in Nigeria continued to be acute.

A World in Turmoil

The political weakness of the new African states, the lack of economic viability of many of them, the ineffectiveness of the Organization of African Unity, and the determined opposition of "hard core" white-dominated areas to African nationalism were some of the factors that contributed to Africa's turmoil. These conditions underlined the uncertainty of Africa's future and made its role in world affairs unpredictable.

. . . .

Disarmament and Arms Control

A central concern of all peoples and nations since the end of World War II has been the nuclear arms race. It has stood as a potent reminder not only of the failure of the international community to establish a sound basis for peace, but of how close the world has been to the possibility of extinction. Although the arms race has been a symptom, rather than the cause, of the world's troubles, reflecting the global tensions that exist, its impact on all societies has been tremendous.

In the modern nation-state system, military power is recognized as an essential ingredient for the protection, well-being, and promotion of a country's national interests. As such it serves as an instrument for the attainment of both the political and economic ends of the state and buttresses diplomacy during peacetime. Where the danger arises is when a nation feels it enjoys a definite superiority or preponderance of power. The temptation is then great, especially in moments of great stress or crisis, to use military power, rather than diplomacy, to resolve a dispute. Because the most basic problem that faces the world today is the prevention of nuclear war, the need to limit—and, one hopes, to abolish—recourse to the use of force has become an urgent necessity.

Although many people view disarmament as the principal means by which this goal can be attained, it is clear that as long as distrust, suspicion, and fear among states continue to prevail, nations will not disarm. Still, statesmen, particularly in the Western world, have traditionally recognized a dual obligation: to defend their own national interests, but at the same time to advance the international "common good" by striving to create

Jules Davids

a world order in which power will be controlled by the rule of law and not by the dictum that "might makes right."

For more than two decades, delegates of the United States, the Soviet Union, and many other countries have met thousands of times, at different levels and places and in different bodies, to discuss various types of disarmament proposals. Although the results of these efforts have been meager, they have not been without significance. To be sure, the arms control agreements concluded in the 1960s have mainly dealt with peripheral problems, but they provide some hope that a major "breakthrough" on disarmament negotiations is possible.

One cannot, however, underestimate the difficulties involved. The primary obstacles to disarmament are not only economic, strategic, and technical, but also, most fundamentally, political in nature. Since the aim of each nation is to increase, and not weaken, its relative power position, it will be wary of disarmament negotiations detrimental to its interests. Such negotiations, in fact, can be a two-edged sword: they can be employed to freeze a status quo, thus preserving and even enhancing the superiority of one country over another; and they can provide a blind, enabling a weaker country to overcome its inferiority through deceptive means....

From the end of World War II to 1970, four phases can be discerned in disarmament negotiations. During the first period, from 1946 to 1955, the principal arena of discussions was in the United Nations. Addressing the first session of the newly established United Nations Atomic Energy Commission in New York on June 14, 1946, Bernard Baruch opened the debate on disarmament and set the stage for ensuing quarrels between the United States and the Soviet Union. To "provide the mechanism to assure that atomic energy is used for peaceful purposes," he proposed the creation of an International Atomic Development Authority within the framework of the United Nations and offered to relinquish America's atomic monopoly, to give the IADA exclusive authority over all stockpiles of nuclear weapons, and to permit it to exercise full rights of inspection and to impose sanctions for violations. The Baruch Plan, however, demanded a foolproof system of control and inspection

A World in Turmoil

before the United States would surrender its atomic bomb monopoly.

Moscow flatly rejected the American proposals. Equating all controls with an infringement on its sovereignty and an open invitation to engage in espionage, the Russians declared that the Baruch Plan was simply an attempt to stop the Soviet Union from acquiring its own independent nuclear weapons and to perpetuate a Western monopoly. The Kremlin insisted that before agreement was reached on controls and inspection, steps had to be taken to ban all nuclear weapons, to destroy all existing nuclear stockpiles, to halt further testing of nuclear weapons, and to dismantle American military bases abroad.

The conflict between the American and Soviet approaches on disarmament persisted until 1955 and produced a deadlock. During the second phase of negotiations, from the spring of 1955 through the spring of 1958, both Moscow and Washington began to modify their positions. They came around to accepting the British and French view on the necessity of "staging," or "phasing," of disarmament procedures, but the United States insisted that each "stage," starting with areas of least sensitivity, be carefully defined and that disarmament be made progressive. A succeeding stage, Washington indicated, would be initiated only after the preceding stage had been satisfactorily completed. There was continued stress on comprehensive disarmament programs, but attention was increasingly directed toward specific measures relating to "arms control" or "partial disarmament."

In the mid-1950s, two issues in particular were singled out: a ban on nuclear testing, and reduction of the danger of possible surprise attacks. A series of nuclear tests conducted by the United States in the Pacific in March 1954, which resulted in a large amount of radioactive fallout, elicited worldwide alarm and criticism. Pressure steadily intensified in the United Nations to stop explosions in the atmosphere, and from 1955 on the problem of ending the testing became a key question of international concern.

Aware of its propaganda value, Moscow immediately identified itself publicly with advocates of a nuclear test ban. Taking

JULES DAVIDS

the initiative to promote this step, the Soviet Union submitted proposals to the United Nations in May 1955. One of the first measures in the first stage of its comprehensive disarmament program was the cessation of nuclear tests. In addition, Moscow urged the reduction of armed forces and conventional armaments, and indicated that if the Soviet plan were adopted, it would be willing to agree to the creation of an International Control Organ (with its own staff of inspectors) that could, "within the bounds of the control functions," have "unimpeded access at all times to all objects of control."

Although Moscow moved cautiously on a test ban, on accepting the West's position on staging, and, within limits, on inspection and control, Washington found itself unprepared for the Soviet démarche. Instead of responding directly to the Soviet plan, the Eisenhower administration expressed its worry about the danger of hidden stockpiles that might not be detected by inspectors, and its fear that the Soviet Union might not abide by a test ban even if agreement could be reached. The United States rejected Moscow's claim that national detection systems were adequate in disclosing violations that might occur, and it refused to consider a test ban that would be separate from other disarmament measures and not subject to effective international controls.

Convinced at this time that a test ban by itself would not end the arms race or halt the spread of nuclear weapons to other powers, Washington shifted its attention to what it considered a more immediate and pressing problem: the creation of an inspection system that would take the surprise out of a possible surprise attack. At the Geneva summit meeting in July 1955, President Eisenhower suggested as one element in this approach the "open skies" plan. He also proposed that air and ground inspection might constitute a comprehensive early-warning system to eliminate the likelihood of surprise attacks. But at the Geneva meeting (and even after that), nothing was said about how to prevent the danger of a surprise missile, atomic submarine, or bomb-carrying satellite attack.

During this second phase of disarmament negotiations, there was major controversy not only over a test ban agreement, but

A World in Turmoil

over the respective stage-by-stage plans offered by Britain, France, Russia, and the United States. Disputes developed on both the order of the stages to be followed and how transitions would be effected from one stage to the next. Efforts to reconcile the conflicting positions were unsuccessful.

In June 1957, however, the Soviet Union again made a bid to separate a test ban from the comprehensive disarmament plans. For the first time, the Soviets agreed to accept a system of inspection and controls to supervise the halting of tests. Recognizing the importance of this concession, the United States and its Western European allies responded promptly by convening experts to draft an inspection system. During the summer Washington indicated its willingness to suspend tests, provided the Russians agreed to cut back also on their nuclear weapons production and permitted inspectors to verify that all fissionable material would be used only for peaceful purposes. The Kremlin rejected these counterproposals. Although it was prepared to consider negotiations on the duration of a test suspension, the Soviet Union would not accept a cutoff of its production of fissionable material for defense purposes unless the West agreed to an absolute ban against the use of all atomic and hydrogen weapons.

No formal agreement was concluded. However, after each of the nuclear powers had completed their series of nuclear tests in 1958, the United States announced that it would voluntarily suspend further testing, pending the completion of a nuclear test ban treaty. No further tests took place in the atmosphere during the next three years.

The third phase of disarmament negotiations, from 1958 to the summer of 1961, was, in many respects, the most critical. In September 1959, Premier Khrushchev, speaking before the U.N. General Assembly, reverted to the goal of total disarmament. "The task," he said, "is to find a lever by grasping which mankind can be stopped from sliding into the ... abyss of war." The Soviet leader then offered a "Declaration of the Soviet Government on General and Complete Disarmament" that proposed to abolish, within four years, all armies, navies, and air forces in the world; to wipe out all military bases on foreign territories; to destroy all atomic and hydrogen bombs and halt their further production; and to eliminate the stockpiles of chemical and bacteriological war materials. "Military rockets of all ranges," Khrushchev declared, "will be liquidated, and rocket facilities will remain only as a means of transportation and for the harnessing of outer space." He argued that, because there would be nothing to control, complete disarmament would end the problem of control.

From the West's viewpoint, the Russian proposals were regarded as little more than a propaganda bid to woo world opinion. Conspicuously lacking in the Soviet "Declaration" were specific details on how its goals were to be attained. The United States pressed vigorously to reduce the intensity of the arms race and continued its efforts to seek a limitation of armaments, but the hope of reconciling the divergent viewpoints between America and her European allies and between the West and the Soviet Union were quashed in the spring of 1960 by the U-2 incident and the Paris meeting debacle.

Early in 1961, President Kennedy made another effort to reach an agreement on a test ban. At the Kennedy-Khrushchev meeting in Vienna that June, however, the Soviet leader expressed little interest; instead he urged taking up the "main, cardinal question—the question of general and complete disarmament," which would automatically solve the problem of nuclear testing as well. The reason for this reversal of tactics soon became apparent.

Three months later, the Soviet Union unilaterally resumed the testing of its nuclear weapons. In September, the Kremlin set off a long series of detonations, obviously prepared long in advance, and for the next several weeks, at one- or two-day intervals, explosions took place in the atmosphere. Because of Khrushchev's violation of the test moratorium, President Kennedy promptly announced that the United States would be compelled to resume its own nuclear tests. These were subsequently undertaken in the Pacific in April 1962, and were followed by a second round of Soviet tests, several of which were in the multimegaton range.

The breakdown of the test moratorium opened a new pe-

A World in Turmoil

riod of intensified nuclear weapons development. On September 25, 1961, President Kennedy, speaking before the U.N. General Assembly, set the stage for the fourth phase of disarmament negotiations. Stressing the need to curb the arms race, he dramatically declared:

> Today, every inhabitant of this planet must contemplate the day when this planet may no longer be habitable. Every man, woman, and child lives under a nuclear sword of Damocles, hanging by the slenderest of threads, capable of being cut at any moment by accident or miscalculation or by madness. The weapons of war must be abolished before they abolish us.
>
> Men no longer debate whether armaments are a symptom or a cause of tension. The mere existence of modern weapons—10 million times more powerful than any that the world has ever seen, and only minutes away from any target on earth—is a source of horror and discord and distrust.
>
> Men no longer maintain that disarmament must await the settlement of all disputes, for disarmament must be part of any permanent settlement. And men may no longer pretend that the quest for disarmament is a sign of weakness, for in a spiraling arms race a nation's security may well be shrinking even as its arms increase.[1]

The president then set forth a five-point program that formed the basis of America's disarmament proposals in the 1960s: (1) the signing of a test ban treaty by all nations; (2) the stopping of production of fissionable materials for war; (3) an agreement on the nonproliferation of nuclear weapons; (4) the banning of nuclear weapons in outer space; and (5) the gradual destruction of existing stockpiles of nuclear weapons, as well as strategic nuclear delivery vehicles. In addition, Kennedy called for the extension of the rules of international law both on earth and to "man's new domain—outer space.... Unless man can match his strides in weaponry and technology with equal strides in social and political development," he said, "our great strength, like that of the dinosaur, will become incapable of proper control and, like the dinosaur, vanish from [the] earth." To empha-

[1] *Documents on American Foreign Relations*, 1961 (New York, 1962), pp. 475–76.

size the top priority the United States intended to place on disarmament, President Kennedy created a new Arms Control and Disarmament Agency to formulate policies in this field and to draft and negotiate a test ban treaty.

What spurred disarmament efforts were the Cuban missile crisis in 1962 and the growing rift between the Soviet Union and Communist China. The Cuban affair was primarily responsible for the establishment of a communications link, or "hot line," that was put into operation on August 30, 1963. Its purpose was to reduce the danger that the two superpowers might misread each other's intentions in some future crisis.

Meanwhile, President Kennedy joined British Prime Minister Harold Macmillan in a special appeal to Khrushchev to undertake new high-level talks on a test ban agreement. "The conclusion of such a treaty—so near and yet so far—would check the spiraling arms race in one of its most dangerous areas," Kennedy declared in a commencement address at American University on June 10. "It would place the nuclear powers in a position to deal more effectively with one of the greatest hazards which man faces in 1963, the further spread of nuclear arms." Noting that Khrushchev had responded favorably to the request for tripartite talks, Kennedy announced that the United States would not conduct any further nuclear tests in the atmosphere "so long as other states do not do so."

During July, W. Averell Harriman, under secretary of state for political affairs, and Viscount Hailsham, lord president of the Council and minister for science in the British government, were sent to Moscow to probe Soviet intentions. Prospects for a test ban agreement were still uncertain, for Khrushchev intimated that it would be dependent on the conclusion of a NATO-Warsaw nonaggression pact. Simultaneously with the tripartite talks, a showdown occurred in the Soviet-Chinese ideological quarrel. Angered at Peking's public polemics, Russia published a full statement on July 14 of its grievances against the Chinese Communist party. This blast resulted in an open split between the two countries and hastened the collapse of private meetings then taking place in Moscow.

At the same time, however, it also facilitated the conclusion

A World in Turmoil

of a test ban treaty. Sidestepping the contentious issues on underground testing and a nonaggression pact, the British and American negotiators and Foreign Minister Andrei Gromyko quickly reached an agreement. On July 25, they initiated the draft of a treaty that prohibited nuclear testing in the atmosphere, in outer space, or underwater.

The Limited Nuclear Test Ban Treaty, the first treaty concluded by the United States with the Soviet Union since World War II, went into effect on October 10, 1963, after it had been ratified by the three original signatories. Although more than a hundred countries later signed the treaty, France and Communist China were conspicuous omissions. Both countries were intent on developing their own nuclear programs, and their refusal to accept the terms of the agreement obviously limited its effectiveness and posed problems for the future. Nevertheless, the treaty was a landmark; it gave promise that other disarmament agreements could be worked out, that the likelihood of war could be reduced. An additional step, in fact, was quickly taken by the U.N. General Assembly on October 17, with a resolution (approved by acclamation) providing for the banning of nuclear weapons in space.

Next, following the Test-Ban Treaty, President Johnson pressed for a cutback in the production of fissionable material for nuclear weapons. In his State of the Union message in January 1964, he announced that the United States would reduce its production by 25 percent and close four plutonium piles. He called on the Soviet Union to do the same.

Seeking to break new ground, Washington also offered to negotiate for the first time a separate agreement for a "verified freeze" on strategic nuclear delivery vehicles—mainly long-range bombers and missiles. This proposal sought to come to grips with the single most critical issue in arms control; for danger of all-out nuclear war hinged not so much on the possession of nuclear warheads, as on the delivery systems that could carry them to targets. Since a "verified freeze" entailed placing missile plants and testing sites under international control, it was rejected by the Soviet Union. The Russians claimed, as they had in connection with the Baruch Plan, that it would simply legalize espionage without reducing armaments and enable a potential aggressor to collect information to launch a sudden blow.

Moscow dismissed President Johnson's idea for a "freeze" as propaganda. In April, however, Khrushchev pledged to cut back substantially the production of U-235 for nuclear weapons, and to allocate more fissionable materials for peaceful purposes. Since both the United States and the Soviet Union had more than enough nuclear materials to meet their weapons requirements, the reductions in no way affected the arms race.

The event that reawakened efforts to restrain the nuclear arms race was China's explosion of an atomic device in October 1964. Both the United States and Britain were especially alarmed over the danger of the possible spread of nuclear weapons to states that did not already have them. It was imperative, they believed, to halt the proliferation before it became too late. In 1965, London drafted a nonproliferation agreement that sought to prohibit "have" nuclear powers from supplying "have not" countries with nuclear weapons or technology and to commit "have not" states not to manufacture or otherwise acquire nuclear weapons on their own initiative.

During the next two years, however, progress on a nonproliferation treaty was stymied. Washington's efforts to develop some form of multilateral sharing with its NATO allies that would include West Germany's participation were a major stumbling block. The Kremlin strenuously objected to all such schemes, bluntly declaring that they would put West Germany's finger on America's nuclear trigger. The demise of the MLF (Multilateral Force) and other multilateral nuclear proposals helped clear the way toward joint cooperation on a nonproliferation treaty. Far more significant, however, was the concern of Washington and Moscow over China's growing nuclear strength.

Late in June 1967, President Johnson met Premier Kosygin at Glassboro, New Jersey. This meeting was primarily for the purpose of discussing problems relating to Israel's Six-Day war and to the Vietnam conflict. Though it merely confirmed the fundamental differences between the two powers on issues in

A World in Turmoil

the Middle East and Vietnam, the Glassboro talks resulted in an important understanding on a nuclear nonproliferation agreement. In August, both countries submitted separate, but identical, drafts of a treaty to the eighteen-nation Disarmament Committee at Geneva. Overwhelmingly approved by the U.N. General Assembly in June 1968, the Nonproliferation Treaty was signed by more than eighty nations, including the United States, the United Kingdom, and the Soviet Union. Although the Senate Foreign Relations Committee endorsed the treaty in September 1968, the United States withheld its formal ratification until March 13, 1969. This delay was caused by the crisis in Czechoslovakia, and by President-elect Nixon's request that no action be taken pending his review of Soviet-American relations.

The Nonproliferation Treaty, like the Limited Nuclear Test Ban, by no means solved all the problems presented by the existence of nuclear weapons. In no way did it affect the existing arsenals in the five countries that already possessed them, nor did it impose any restraints on their continued development and production of nuclear weapons. Moreover, the refusal of France and China to sign the treaty left a serious loophole. The heavy majority that favored the agreement, however, believed it would deter other countries from embarking on new national nuclear weapons programs....

TODAY AND TOMORROW:
THE CHALLENGES THAT LIE AHEAD

The 1960s may well be a watershed not only in America's history, but for the future of mankind. Whether it will be possible to meet the awesome challenges of our technological age remains uncertain. Much will depend on the capacity of peoples to harness the resources of physical and human power toward the eradication of social and economic inequities and the elimination of political oppression. The past decade has sharply disclosed the magnitude of these problems.

For the United States, these years have been marked by continual crises both at home and abroad—the tragic assassinations of John F. Kennedy, Martin Luther King, and Robert F.

Jules Davids

Kennedy; racial strife, riots, and violence in the streets; and the rise of black power and student radicalism on campuses of colleges and universities throughout the country. While tensions in American life were, in part, an outward manifestation of the turmoil in the world community, they were also a product of a deeper malaise that arose from doubts about the values and premises rooted in American society.

These doubts were reflected most particularly in a questioning of the basic objectives and purposes of American policies and the ends to which power was being used. The Vietnam War intensified the mood of frustration and disillusionment, but the sources of discontent were also the result of fundamental differences over policy priorities, the excessive influence of the military-industrial complex, and America's role as a responsible world leader.

Among the disheartening trends observable in the 1960s has been the increased fragmentation both within countries and in the world community. Although regional economic integration has achieved some success, little headway has been made politically. Many reasons account for this situation.

Significant in this regard is the heritage of World War II. The absence of an overall peace settlement contributed to a scramble between the United States and the Soviet Union for a controlling influence in various parts of the world: in Eastern Europe, in Germany, and in Asia and the Far East. A pattern emerged in which temporary armistice lines were converted into de facto partitions. Such lines were drawn not only in Germany, Korea, and Indochina, but in the Middle East (dividing the new state of Israel from neighboring Arab countries), and in the Formosa Straits, Kashmir, and Cyprus....

A reversal in the process of fragmentation, in the closing of the gap between rich and poor countries, and in the halting of the nuclear arms race and the attainment of genuine disarmament will be possible only when nation-states begin to look beyond their own self-interests to the common interests of all peoples and to the means by which their differences can be resolved. Unfortunately, this day has not yet come. But the pressures of today may make this age-old dream a reality tomorrow.

CHAPTER 7

The Constitutional Right to Privacy: From GRISWOLD to ROE V. WADE and Beyond

WALTER I. GILES

Counting his undergraduate and graduate student years, Jack Giles was part of the School of Foreign Service community for over fifty of its seventy-five years. Many thousands of Georgetown students studied political science with him from 1947 to 1990, including an appreciative future president. Those in his popular constitutional law classes in later years will recognize this lecture, later added to their casebook reading for the course. Drawn from several lectures by Professor Giles on the rise and development of the constitutional right to privacy, this one offers up the contemporary appeal, intrinsic interest, and continuing controversial development of its subject, as well as a cool approach to a hot topic.

The Constitutional Right to Privacy

FROM *GRISWOLD* (1965) TO *ROE* (1973): AN OVERVIEW

Substantive due process, *Lochner*-style, which developed in the late nineteenth century and flourished for five decades thereafter, was repudiated by the Supreme Court in a number of decisions, beginning especially in 1937 with *West Coast Hotel Co. v. Parrish*. Within a few years of *West Coast Hotel*, Lochnerism had been thoroughly discredited as an appropriate constitutional doctrine. In a number of cases, decided after 1937, the justices would refer to "the demise of substantive due process doctrine, *Lochner*-style." For example, Justice Black writing for the Court in *Ferguson v. Skrupa* (1963) observed:

> The doctrine that prevailed in *Lochner, Coppage, Adkins, Burns*, and like cases—that due process authorizes courts to hold laws unconstitutional when they believe the legislature has acted unwisely—has long since been discarded. We have returned to the original constitutional proposition that courts do not substitute their social and economic beliefs for the judgment of legislative bodies, who are elected to pass laws.
>
> . . . . .
>
> We refuse to sit as a "superlegislature to weigh the wisdom of legislation," and we emphatically refuse to go back to the time when courts used the due process clause "to strike down state laws, regulatory of business and industrial conditions, because they may be unwise, improvident, or out of harmony with a particular school of thought."

Yet, as scholars such as Professor Gunther have noted, substantive due process principles, developed during the *Lochner* era, did survive the 1937 constitutional revolution. A number

Walter I. Giles

of substantive due process decisions involving *individual liberties* (or what are sometimes called today *human rights*), as distinct from property rights (or liberties), handed down during the Lochner era maintained their vitality after 1937. See, for example, *Meyer v. Nebraska* (1923) and *Pierce v. Society of Sisters* (1925).

Even after 1937, the official date for the repudiation of substantive due process, the Court decided in 1942 the case of *Skinner v. Oklahoma*, an equal protection case but very similar to substantive due process determination.[1] All of these cases proved to be building blocks that the contemporary Supreme Court has used in its revival of substantive due process jurisprudence and its resort to what is called "non-interpretive" review.[2]

The privacy and personal liberty adjudication of the Court constitutes the most significant component in the justices' revival of substantive due process principles of constitutional law.[3] And it is this adjudication, dominated to a great extent by the landmark and controversial decision in *Roe v. Wade* (1973), that has engendered so much debate among commentators, the bar, the bench, and political actors, concerning the legitimacy of the Court's contemporary substantive due process rulings.

The modern story begins with *Griswold v. Connecticut* (1965). In *Griswold* the Court first articulated a constitutional right of privacy (specifically it was a right of *marital privacy*), a right nowhere found in the Constitution, nor could it easily be implied from any particular right found in the text. Locating the constitutional source of this right of marital privacy was exceedingly difficult, especially for a Court which had unambiguously rejected substantive due process principles for some thirty years.

Justice Douglas wrote for the Court in *Griswold* in an opinion reflecting some highly creative principles of constitutional law. Critics contended that his constitutional analysis was at least bizarre, even if not woven from whole cloth. Douglas conceded that there was no right of marital privacy *per se* in the Constitution and that there was no one specific guarantee in the document from which such a right could be implied. But he reasoned that a right of marital privacy could be derived

The Constitutional Right to Privacy

from the *penumbras* of several specific constitutional rights which reflected various kinds of privacy interests and values.[4] These various penumbras collectively coalesce and form a specific constitutional right of marital privacy.

Through this kind of ingenious legal analysis, Justice Douglas believed the Court had avoided the criticism that the judges were going back to the discredited doctrinal principles of substantive due process and once again creating, and reading into the Constitution, "rights" nowhere found in the document but which, however, seemed important or fundamental from the perspective of the individual justices' social or economic philosophical predilections.

The two dissenters in *Griswold*, Justices Black and Stewart, would have none of the Douglas penumbral formulation and in very strong language they made it clear that what the Court was doing here was creating a right of privacy by resorting to substantive due process (or "natural law" principles, as Black often expressed it). Before launching into an extraordinarily vigorous dissent, Justice Black said from the bench: "I am letting it be known today that this is no ordinary decision." Black warned of the dangers of what the Court was doing. He argued that the justices must confine their authority to specific provisions of the Constitution and not set up the Court as a kind of superlegislature, approving or nullifying laws on the basis of whether the justices thought they were "unwise or unnecessary" as it had done during the Lochner era.

Black severely attacked the majority opinion of Justice Douglas, contending it was nothing less than an exercise of substantive due process, despite its base in penumbral theory and its reliance, in part, on the Ninth Amendment. The Court, he argued, was in effect reviving a legal doctrine that most of the sitting justices at the time had professed to reject on the ground that it (substantive due process) constituted illegitimate constitutional policy-making by the Court.

ROE V. WADE AND BEYOND

Although the *Griswold* Court used the penumbral theory to discover or create a constitutional right of privacy, the Court never subsequently grounded any of its privacy decisions on this rather artificial theory of constitutional interpretation. Rather, the Court as a whole shifted its privacy rights jurisprudence squarely to a substantive due process methodology. It did so in its major, and most controversial, privacy right case, *Roe v. Wade* (1973). There the Court, speaking through Justice Blackmun, held that a woman had the right, as a federal constitutional right of privacy, to decide the question of terminating her own pregnancy.

What is the constitutional source of this particular privacy right? Said Justice Blackmun:

> This right of privacy, whether it be founded in the Fourteenth Amendment's concept of personal liberty and restrictions upon state action, as we feel it is, or, as the District Court determined, in the Ninth Amendment's reservation of rights to the people, is broad enough to encompass a woman's decision whether or not to terminate her pregnancy.

The *Roe* Court, therefore, made it clear that whatever rights of constitutional privacy existed derived directly from the "liberty" protected by the due process clauses of the Fourteenth and Fifth Amendments.[5] This *ipse dixit* was unequivocally the result of substantive due process methodology, although the Blackmun opinion in *Roe* did not characterize it as such.

But Justice Stewart did so in his concurring opinion in *Roe*. Stewart had dissented in *Griswold* but he now accepted the *Griswold* holding, as well as *Roe's*. And Stewart made it clear that what he was now accepting was an exercise of substantive due process. It was clear to him in *Griswold*, he said, and now, in *Roe*, "equally clear" that the *Griswold* decision "can be rationally understood only as a holding that the Connecticut statute substantively invaded the 'liberty' that is protected by the Due Process Clause of the Fourteenth Amendment. As so understood *Griswold* stands as one in a long line of pre-*Skrupa* cases decided under the doctrine of substantive due process, and I now accept it as such."

The Dissents of Justices White and Rehnquist. Justice White and Justice Rehnquist entered strong dissents in *Roe*. Said Justice White of the Court's ruling:

The Constitutional Right to Privacy

> I find nothing in the language or history of the Constitution to support the Court's judgment. The Court simply fashions and announces a new constitutional right for pregnant mothers and, with scarcely any reason or authority for its action, invests that right with sufficient substance to override most existing state abortion statutes [by adopting the compelling interest test].
>
> . . . . .
>
> As an exercise of raw judicial power, the Court perhaps has authority to do what it does today; but in my view its judgment is an improvident and extravagant exercise of the power of judicial review that the Constitution extends to this Court.

Justice Rehnquist agreed with Justice White and went on to argue that the Court was, in effect, reviving the long-since discredited doctrine of *Lochner* substantive due process. He focused on the Court's declaration (in Justice Blackmun's opinion) that the privacy right was a "fundamental" constitutional right and that, accordingly, the appropriate standard of review involving its application was the very rigorous test of strict scrutiny and "compelling interest."

> As in *Lochner* and similar cases applying substantive due process standards to economic and social welfare legislation, the adoption of the compelling state interest standard will inevitably require this Court to examine the legislative policies and pass on the wisdom of these policies in the very process of deciding whether a particular state interest put forward may or may not be "compelling."

The Commentators' Reaction to ROE. The *Roe* decision quickly engendered what has become a continuing constitutional and political controversy concerning the legitimacy of the Supreme Court's substantive due process decisions and its occasional resort to non-interpretive review. While many commentators approved of the *result* in *Roe* (the constitutional right of a pregnant woman to decide on an abortion), many also found the reasoning of Justice Blackmun unpersuasive or were troubled by the Court's bold revival of substantive due process principles of constitutional law.

Walter I. Giles

John Hart Ely, a scholar who had favored some kind of a right to an abortion (grounded either in federal or state law), was nonetheless dismayed by Justice Blackmun's opinion in *Roe*. "... *Roe*," he observed, "lacks even colorable support in the constitutional text, history, or any other appropriate source of constitutional doctrine...."[6] And although *Roe v. Wade* seemed likely to be a "durable decision," it was, according to Ely, "nevertheless, a very bad decision. Not because it will perceptibly weaken the Court—it won't; and not because it conflicts with either my [Ely's] idea of progress or what the evidence suggests is society's—it doesn't; ... [but] because it is bad constitutional law, or rather because it is *not* constitutional law and gives almost no sense of an obligation to try to be."[7]

The Debate over the Determination of "Fundamental Rights" Embedded in the Due Process Clause

Ely wrote his now-classic comment on *Roe* because, as he expressed it, the dissents of Justices White and Rehnquist were, in his opinion, not adequate in signaling with any "particular conviction that *Roe* represents an important or unusually dangerous constitutional development."[8] In time a virtual library of scholarship has emerged, largely in the law reviews, dealing with the Court's contemporary revival of substantive due process doctrines and its resort to non-interpretive review.

As the debate has continued, the Court as a whole and individual justices, in dissenting or concurring opinions, have begun to address the subject, especially the particular point of controversy: the determination of specific "fundamental" rights not found in the text of the Constitution. Questions such as the following were raised both by commentators and, at times, by individual justices: How are we to identify those fundamental societal values of our time which are to be read into the Constitution through judicial interpretation? Where are the sources for discovering them? By whom are these fundamental societal values to be identified and then "constitutionalized"? By elected officials? By nonelected, appointed-for-life, nonaccountable justices of the Supreme Court? Questions such as these go to the heart of representative government.

The Constitutional Right to Privacy

Endnotes

1. That opinion, written by Justice Douglas, recognized marriage and procreation as "fundamental" and among the "basic civil rights of man." *Skinner* was a forerunner of the "fundamental interests" branch of the "new" equal protection. Gunther has described this 1942 reference in *Skinner* as "extraordinary." He points out that this decision "mixing due process and equal protection considerations, was virtually the only one in that period between the demise of *Lochner* [1937] and *Griswold* [1965] to exercise special scrutiny in favor of a 'fundamental liberty' not tied to a specific constitutional guarantee." (Gerald Gunther, *Constitutional Law*, 11th ed. [Mineola, N.Y.: Foundation Press, 1985], 503.)

2. "A long-standing dispute in constitutional theory has gone under different names at different times; but today's terminology seems as helpful as any. Today we are likely to call the contending sides 'interpretivism' and 'noninterpretivism'—the former indicating that judges deciding constitutional issues should confine themselves to enforcing norms that are stated or clearly implicit in the written Constitution, the latter the contrary view that courts should go beyond that set of references and enforce norms that cannot be discovered within the four corners of the document." (John Hart Ely, *Democracy and Distrust: A Theory of Judicial Review* [Cambridge, Mass.: Harvard University Press, 1980], 1.)

3. The Court did resort to substantive due process *methodology* in its significant nationalization of the federal Bill of Rights between 1925 and 1971. By its expanded interpretation, on a case-by-case basis, of the word "liberty" in the Fourteenth Amendment's due process clause, the justices eventually "incorporated" virtually all of the guarantees of the federal Bill of Rights—all of the major ones except one—into the due process clause, thus making those guarantees applicable against the States (hence, the term "nationalization of the Bill of Rights"). Although this process of judicial interpretation used a substantive due process methodology (reading new rights into the "liberty" concept of the Fourteenth Amendment's due process clause), it was different from both the *Lochner* freedom-of-contract substantive due process and the contemporary privacy-and-personal-liberty due process adjudication of the Court in that the specific rights so incorporated into the Fourteenth Amendment were already in the text of the Constitution (they existed as specific guarantees in the Bill of Rights, enforceable against the *federal* government).

4. Douglas cited specifically certain guarantees in the First, Third, Fourth, Fifth, and Ninth Amendments, the penumbras of which protected some kind of individual privacy from governmental intrusion. These penumbral emanations collectively came together and formed a zone of privacy that in turn encompassed the marriage relationship.

5. The Fourteenth Amendment due process clause (". . . nor shall any State deprive any person of life, liberty, or property, without due process of law . . .") applies only to the States; the Fifth Amendment due process clause (". . . nor shall any person . . . be deprived of life, liberty, or property, without due process of law. . .") applies to the federal government.

6. Ely, "The Wages of Crying Wolf: A Comment on *Roe v. Wade*," 82 *Yale L. J.* 920, 943 (1973).

7. Ibid. at 947.

8. Ibid. at 920, n. 3.

CHAPTER 8

"Passive Agent of Omnipotent Capital": The Entrepreneur in Marxian Theory

Joseph Zrinyi, S.J.

> Great-nephew of a famous Hungarian resistance figure, Father Zrinyi was European to the core and regularly shepherded Georgetown students to the continent in summer. Noted for his remarkable memory (and his anti-Marxist humor), he taught the principles of economics enthusiastically, some said almost religiously. The students rewarded his loving discipline by repeatedly voting him their favorite teacher. These 1969 comments by Father Zrinyi on the fate of Marxism in Central Europe might almost have been written in 1989.
>
> SOURCE: "The Entrepreneur in the Marxian System," *Documentation sur l'Europe Centrale* (Louvain), Vol. VII, No. 1, 1969, pp. 3–9.

"Passive Agent of Omnipotent Capital"

A spectre is haunting the Marxist societies in Central Europe, the spectre of individualism and entrepreneurial spirit. All the powers of the Communist Establishment have entered into holy alliance to exorcise this spectre—the dynamic factor of socioeconomic life, imbued with a restless, creative spirit, a personal free agent.

By breaking away from routine, this spirit subjects societies and economies to continuous change and development. Werner Sombart called it the personification of the European soul. Its creative freedom has ostensibly begun to undermine the Marxian edifice.

Indeed, Marx's misconception of the entrepreneur may be the weakest point of his system. His theory of entrepreneurship is intimately connected with his dependence on the English classics, especially on Ricardo, and on the Hegelian method of explaining socioeconomic change.[1]

The Impact of Hegel and Ricardo

Schumpeter makes the students of Marxism beware of overstressing the Hegelian influence on Marx, arguing that "his vision of the capitalist process as a whole may be either traced to sources other than philosophical—such as Ricardo's economic theory—or else understood as the results of a strictly empirical analysis of his own."[2] In Schumpeter's view, Marx's theory of economic change developed independently of his Hegelian affiliation, so that Hegel's influence upon him was not more than "phraseological."

With all respect to Schumpeter, we are inclined to think that he unduly minimizes the substantive connexion between Hegel and Marx. The constant references by Marx, Engels, and Lenin to the fact that Marxism is the legitimate successor of German philosophy (Fichte, Hegel, Feuerbach) and to the "materialistic inversion" of the Hegelian dialectic lead us to the conclusion that Hegel's influence upon Marx was more than "phraseological."[3]

Hegel's philosophy is the most daring attempt to establish a principle as the source of unity and diversity, or multiplicity. His concept of the Absolute, as a concrete Idea, contains both of these aspects: a single ultimate principle and an observable multiplicity as it unfolds, by virtue of its own laws of development, following the celebrated "dialectic" process.

Lenin's enthusiasm for Hegel's scheme as a "work of genius" and as "an idea of world-embracing, universal, living interconnexion of all things one with another" illustrates Hegel's powerful attraction for Marxist thinkers. The revolutionary dialectic method, the advance beyond negation to the negation of the negation, the immense power of synthesis—all belong to the substance of Marxian interpretation of reality. What Marxism did was to construct a framework along Hegelian lines by transforming the "idealistic dialectic" into a "materialistic" one, according to which, then, socioeconomic change takes place.

Schumpeter's emphasis on the dependence of Marx's economics on the Ricardian school is more convincing.[4] In Schumpeter's view, Ricardo's labor-quantity theory of value suggested Marx's full use of it in applying it to labor itself. But Ricardo may have suggested that he also considered surplus value as a costless gain for the capitalist. In Ricardo's reasoning, following Adam Smith, a capitalist—being a capitalist (conceptually not distinguished from the entrepreneur) simply by furnishing the workers with tools, materials, and means of subsistence—receives these "advances" back with profit, which obviously resulted in part from the workers' labor.

Hegelian method and Ricardian economics are thus the framework within which the Marxian theory of socioeconomic change should be placed and which, in turn, is the setting for the Marxian theory of entrepreneurship.

"Passive Agent of Omnipotent Capital"

CHANGE ACCORDING TO MARXIAN THEORY

Marx's theory of change has two characteristic bases: (a) that social reality consists of a specified set of relations; (b) that the same reality is in a process of change, following the Hegelian dialectic, inherent in these relations.

Society is seen by Marx as a set of relations, or a framework, made up of two elements: a basis and a superstructure. His clearest formulation of such a social framework was given in the preface to *A Contribution of the Critique of Political Economy*.[5] There he defines the *basis* of society as the "economic structure," consisting of the aggregate of the productive relationships that correspond to a definite stage of development of the material productive forces. Man enters into any such stage of development independently of his will. The *superstructure* is conceived as the sphere of legal relations, political life, philosophical, aesthetic, and religious ideas, with which definite forms of social consciousness are associated. In his words: "The mode of production in material life determines the general character of the social, political and spiritual process of life."[6]

In the basis, or "economic structure," Marx further distinguishes conceptually two inseparable elements, namely, the "material productive forces," or strictly economic forces, and social "relationships of production," which in turn are simply the legal expression of property relationships developed in the superstructure. "Forces," further, refers to the laborers and the means of production united in a manner characteristic of every stage of economic development. "Relationships" point to the existing structure of social classes established as a function of the economic "forces." These two elements, namely the "economic forces" and "social relationships," are related to each other as "content" and "form": in social production "content" is provided by the productive "forces," and "form" by the "relations" of production.[7]

The dialectical unity between "content" and "form" may endure for a certain period of time under exceptional conditions. In that case social relations are in a peaceful harmony with the forces of production. This harmony is rather theoretical than real, on account of an ever-present interplay between "forces" and "relations." Though social conscience fully develops only in the sphere of superstructure, there are unconscious, instinctive aspirations in the base also, nurtured by philosophical ideas. Because of this dialectical contradiction in the infrastructure, the whole social edifice is in constant movement and fermentation. Then, there comes a moment when the existing "relations" of production change under the pressure of the "forces" of production. This pressure, thus, has originated in the interaction of "the material revolution in the economic condition of production" and the unconscious aspirations in the society.[8]

The superstructure resists the pressure coming from the basis; but the "forces," using a fully conscious class as their vehicle, break into it and overthrow the political power that legally sanctioned the former social relations. Thus the harmony between "content" and "form" has been disturbed by socioeconomic elements; as a result, a change takes place in the superstructure. In Marx's words: "With the change in the economic foundation the whole vast superstructure is more or less rapidly transformed."[9]

This is, in short, Marx's vision of the changing socioeconomic reality. Since it starts out with the principle that the mode of production of material things conditions social and political development and man's intellectual activities are nothing more than a reflection of these economic and social processes in the consciousness of social man, it is properly called a materialist interpretation of history.

How does this vision apply to capitalism and what is the part of the entrepreneur in this change? We turn to these problems now.

Change in a Capitalist Economy, According to Marx

Marx's analysis of change in a capitalist type of production begins with an outline of a noncapitalist exchange economy of small producers in which each one owns his own means of production. In this type of economy producers are motivated by

"Passive Agent of Omnipotent Capital"

the immediate satisfaction of their manifold wants. They carry out production with the aim of exchanging their products with other similarly motivated producers. The exchange, or "metamorphosis of commodity," takes place in two phases: commodity is turned into money and money once again into commodity. This transaction is expressed by the familiar formula: C - M - C (Commodity - Money - Commodity).[10]

A capitalist type of economy essentially differs from this "simple commodity production" economy. The distinguishing character of capitalism is the fact that the ownership of the means of production is vested in one group of individuals while work is performed by another. No production can take place in such a system unless labor power is bought and sold.

In the former case, the circuit C - M - C starts with one commodity and finishes with another. The rationale of this circuit lies in the fact that the commodity acquired through such a "metamorphosis" is qualitatively different from that given up. The underlying factor in the operation is consumption.[11]

In the capitalist type economy this circuit starts with money and ends with more money. The rationale of this operation is that money is quantatively larger at the end than it was in the beginning. In other words, the leading motive in this transaction is to buy means of production (labor and "objective materials") at a certain price and to sell them at a higher price than the capital outlay. Thus the formula for this process becomes: M - C - M + M.[12]

There emerges, thus, an increment from this transaction in the sum drawn out as compared with the sum advanced. The capitalist pays out a certain sum of money, converts it into commodities, and then—with or without an intermediate process of production—converts these back into more money. *Whence comes this increment, or "surplus value,"* as Marx calls it?

It was made possible by the fact the capitalist finds on the market a commodity, namely labor-power, "whose actual consumption is itself an embodiment of labor, and consequently, a creation of value."[13] Marx's solution, then, is that there is one commodity whose value in use possesses the peculiar property of being a source of exchange value. This commodity is labor-power. It is by trading in this commodity that the capitalist obtains the surplus value.

The way he obtains it may be put like this. Labor (or labor-power of the workman) is in a capitalist society a commodity. Therefore its value is equal to the number of labor hours embodied in it, that is, the "socially necessary" amount of labor hours to rear, train, feed, and house the worker. Suppose that this labor quantity equals four hours a day. This would be sufficient to replace the value of all the goods that went to the laborer. If the capitalist buying this labor-power makes him work six hours a day, the product of two additional hours is a surplus value for which he does not give compensation.

Surplus value, therefore, according to Marx, is due to the fact that the capitalist makes the laborer work for him part of the day without paying him for it. In his words: "All surplus value is in substance the embodiment of unpaid working time."[14] The appropriation of surplus value by the capitalist is what Marx calls the "exploitation" of the worker.

Once the creation of surplus value has started, the capitalist's concern will be to expand his capital. His aim will be to appropriate more and more surplus value and to convert at least a portion of it into additional capital. The greatest amount of surplus value, and consequently the greatest power to accumulate, goes to the capitalist who employs the most advanced and efficient technical methods. Under the pressure of competition, then, the introduction of labor-saving devices, new techniques, and mechanization becomes universal.

Marx calls this process *the change in the organic composition of capital*, that is, the use of more and more constant capital (such as machines) and less and less variable capital (labor or wage capital). In other words, during this generalized process of mechanization, the ratio of the capitalist's outlay on materials and machines to total outlay displays a steadily rising trend. This indisputable fact has great consequences in the capitalist system according to Marx; from it he deduced his "law of the falling tendency of the rate of profit."[15]

To the capitalist the important ratio is the rate of profit, in other words the ratio between surplus value and total capital

"Passive Agent of Omnipotent Capital"

outlay (constant plus variable), that is, $s/(c + v)$. For purposes of theoretical analysis, the rate of profit must be looked upon as depending upon the two variables, the rate of surplus value and the organic composition of capital. Once we accept the three Marxian propositions—that (a) in the course of economic development the value of constant capital increases faster than the value of variable capital, (b) only variable capital produces surplus value, and (c) the rate of surplus value in relation to total capital remains constant—then the logical conclusion is that the rate of profit as a percentage of total capital will fall.

A further consequence of this law is even more important for Marx, since it introduces us to the most fundamental characteristic of the capitalist system. Under the pressure of competition among capitalists and under the ever-present menace of the falling tendency of the rate of profit, capitalism becomes "essentially a process of accumulation" or "a continuous conversion of surplus value into capital."[16]

THE MARXIAN ENTREPRENEUR-CAPITALIST

The clustering of these factors constitutes the immanent laws of capitalist production. The place and role of the entrepreneur must be searched for within these laws. Given these laws it becomes evident that the capitalist entrepreneur is nothing but a *passive agent* for an anonymous power. What has been for Adam Smith the "invisible hand" becomes for Marx the automatic process of accumulation from which the personal element—or the free agent—in the economic process is completely eliminated.

Further study of Marxian thought confirms this assertion. For Marx the anonymous capital is the compelling and determining power in the economy, having its own laws "not only independent of human will, consciousness and intelligence, but rather on the contrary, determining that will."[17] This impersonal factor is "working with iron necessity toward inevitable results."[18] The capitalist aiming at profit-making alone in a restless, never-ending process is nothing but "capital personified."[19] As such, he is only one of the wheels of a social mechanism:

> The development of capitalist production makes it

constantly necessary to keep increasing the amount of the capital laid out in a given industrial undertaking, and competition makes the immanent laws of capitalist production to be felt by each individual capitalist, as external coercive laws. It compels him to keep constantly extending his capital, in order to preserve it, but extend he cannot, except by means of progressive accumulation.[20]

From the preceding it becomes apparent that the actions of the capitalist are the mere functions of capital; he is not a free agent in any sense. His behavior and his motives are given by his social status in production, which he occupies independently of his will. The fact that he is motivated exclusively not by the creation of values in use and the enjoyment of them, but by the creation and accumulation of exchange value (surplus values) is not of his own choosing. He is trapped into it by the "objective factors of social mechanism" or by the anonymous driving forces of history.

This is, in short, the setting within which the Marxian entrepreneur operates. The Marxian thought develops along the line of reasoning of Adam Smith and Ricardo, but there are some new aspects in his theory. From his affiliation with the English classics it follows that he does not differentiate a capitalist from an entrepreneur. The latter has no place in his system at all.

In his scheme of thought centering around capitalist development through the laws of production, the capitalist system consists of three classes: "the society of producers," laborers, and "the unproductive consumers." This latter class is irrelevant since everything turns around the laws of production.[21]

The "society of producers" must, further, be conceptually distinguished from the "mere owners" of the means of production. The Marxian entrepreneur-capitalist belongs to the former category. The mere fact of owning capital makes a man neither a capitalist nor an entrepreneur. To be a capitalist and entrepreneur, in his sense, it is necessary to use capital actively, that is, to engage in buying labor power.[22]

The Marxian entrepreneur-capitalist depends in his behavior on the automatic working of capital and is nothing but the representative of capital in action.[23] His function is associated

"Passive Agent of Omnipotent Capital"

"objectively" with exploitation and accumulation of surplus value. Capital cannot perform its automatic function unless it is intimately connected with such a person.

This personified capital performs in everyday life a function of superintendence of the laborers.[24] The entrepreneur-capitalist is like "the conductor of an orchestra"[25] whose task is to impose harmony between himself and the laborers. This function, however, is to be attributed to him not on account of his talents and abilities, but on account of his position in the bourgeois society and the capitalistic productive process.

In such a society the leader of industry (entrepreneur-capitalist) is also a capitalist, for "it is not because he is a leader of industry that a man is [a] capitalist; on the contrary, he is a leader of industry because he is a capitalist."[26]

With this most revealing statement Marx makes his position clear; leadership in industry is a derivative of capital. The Marxian entrepreneur is nothing but the agent of capital in action. He is not a free agent in the economic process nor a producer in any real sense but rather a buyer and consumer of labor-power the use of which produces surplus value for him.

In this capacity he is by definition an exploiter of the workers. In order to increase surplus value, under the impact of competition, he speeds up mechanization. Technical inventions and their application are, then, not due to any personal initiative but rather to the blind mechanism of expanding accumulation. The internal laws of the production process and capital accumulation are the exclusive factors of progress and economic change; *the entrepreneur is relegated to the role of a passive agent of omnipotent capital.*

The Marxian entrepreneur is neither Say's "combiner" of the factors of production, nor the calculating head of a business dealing with such heterogeneous social forces as workers, customers, and suppliers, directing them toward one goal. To Marx the only heterogeneity in the capitalist society is expressed by the antagonism between the two classes; the entrepreneurs, as

Joseph Zrinyi, S.J.

a homogeneous class, are by their social position subjected to the anonymous forces of history.

Nor does the Marxian entrepreneur display the Schumpeterian individual personality, with his innovating abilities, fighting obstacles and assuming risks in his undertaking. Between the static entrepreneur of Say and the dynamic, revolutionary entrepreneur of Schumpeter we find the passive, evolutionary entrepreneur of Marx, incarnating the inner contradictions of capitalism. His role is not to break through obstacles and social barriers but to submit himself to the automatically working and evolving economic forces.

Recent events in Central Europe (even in Russia) indicate that Marx, the ideologist of all times, misread the facts of life.

"Passive Agent of Omnipotent Capital"

ENDNOTES

1. Clearly the most outstanding general studies of Marxian philosophy and economics are E. Boehm von Bawerk, *Karl Marx and the Close of His System* (New York: A. M. Kelley, 1949); J. Y. Calvez, *La Penseé de Karl Marx* (Paris: Ed. du Seuil, 1956); J. Robinson, *An Essay on Marxian Economics* (New York: MacMillan, 1952); P. M. Sweezy, *The Theory of Capitalist Development* (New York: Oxford University Press, 1942). The standard work on "the Hegelian aspects" of Marxism is G. A. Wetter, *Dialectical Materialism*, P. Heath trans. (New York: Praeger, 1958). For an analysis of the Marxian entrepreneur, see especially A. C. Taymans, *L'Homme, Agent de Développement Economique* (Louvain: E. Nauwelaerts, 1951), pp. 190–282, and his article "Marx's Theory of the Entrepreneur," *American Journal of Economics and Sociology* XI (October 1951), pp. 75–90.

2. J. A. Schumpeter, *History of Economic Analysis* (New York: Oxford University Press, 1954), p. 414.

3. Wetter, *Dialectical Materialism*, pp. 3–7.

4. Schumpeter, *History of Economic Analysis*, pp. 596–98, 648–49, 681–85.

5. K. Marx, *A Contribution to the Critique of Political Economy*, trans. I. Stone (New York: International Library Publ. Co., 1904), pp. 9–15.

6. Ibid., p. 11.

7. Wetter, *Dialectical Materialism*, p. 402.

8. Taymans reminds us of the "mystical core" of dialectical materialism by pointing to the substantive role played by a society's philosophical ideas and unconscious aspirations in forming and transforming its infrastructure. In Marx's view the ideas and slogans of the philosophers have the important role of creating a more and more conscious appreciation of the antagonism between the "forces" of production and "social relationships." In the critical moment when these ideas have fully permeated and penetrated the imagination and emotions of the proletarian masses, a qualitative change will take place in the socioeconomic relations breaking up both the basis and the superstructure. (Taymans, *L'Homme*, pp. 223–24.)

9. Marx, *Contribution to the Critique of Political Economy*, p. 372.

10. K. Marx, *Capital*, 3 vols. (Moscow: Foreign Languages Publishing House, 1958), Vol. I., pp. 103–14.

11. Ibid., I, p. 151.

12. Ibid., I, pp. 152–55.

13. Ibid, I, p.167.

14. Ibid., I, p. 534.

15. Ibid., III, pp. 207–35.

16. Ibid., I, pp. 579–88.

17. Ibid., I, p. 18.

18. Ibid., I, p. 8.

19. Ibid., I, p. 152; 591–92.

20. Ibid., I, p. 592.

21. Ibid., III, p. 479.

22   Ibid., III, p. 367.
23   Ibid., III, p. 366, 376.
24   Ibid., III, pp. 370–79.
25   Ibid., III, p. 379.
26   Ibid., I, p. 365.

CHAPTER 9

Joseph A. Schumpeter Revisited

GEORGE J. VIKSNINS

Georgetown students over three decades well recall the lectures from which Professor Viksnins drew this piece, originally written in 1975 and now with a 1994 epilogue. His lecture on Marx and Schumpeter has become the opening salvo to each year's new class of East and Central European Pew Economic Freedom Fellows. Readers will also appreciate learning that Dr. Viksnins has been director of Georgetown's Institute for Comparative Political and Economic Systems since 1982. As senior adviser to the Bank of Latvia since August 1992, he is the godfather of the new Latvian currency, the *lats*.

SOURCES: George J. Viksnins, "Joseph A. Schumpeter: Lover, Horseman, Economist," *National Review*, August 1975, and a "Postscript" written in early 1994.

Joseph A. Schumpeter Revisited

Many years have passed since Joseph A. Schumpeter delivered his last scholarly paper, "The March into Socialism," at the 1949 annual meeting of the American Economic Association in New York. Born in 1883, the same year as John Maynard Keynes, during his lifetime Schumpeter was often referred to as "one of the two greatest living economists." As Daniel R. Fusfeld said in *The Age of the Economist* (1972): "Since his death, economic theory has developed in directions other than those taken by Schumpeter, but economists will continue to consider his three major works as valuable historical and theoretical sources."

To some of us at least, the very fact that Schumpeter is seldom cited and even more rarely read by the current generation of economists bears ironic witness to the power of his analysis. In the autumn of his life, Professor Schumpeter was fond of recalling that he had set himself three goals—to become a great lover, a great horseman, and a great economist. Because he claimed he had only attained two out of three, I offer this brief appreciation.

The Schumpeterian system as a whole is very much beyond our scope here. He himself maintained that a man's fundamental vision of the world and any contributions of real significance to his chosen field were usually complete by the time he reached the age of thirty. Thus, his *Theory of Economic Development* (first published in German in 1911, when Schumpeter was 28) contains the basic outline of his system of analysis.

The focus is on the entrepreneur—the innovator-businessman who seizes upon an idea, a new and better way of doing things, and makes his fortune by putting this idea into practice. Entrepreneurial motivation is the key to capitalistic progress. Many other writers, from Karl Marx to Max Weber, have recognized this—as in Weber's famous phrase, "Accumulate, accumulate, accumulate, that is Moses and the prophets!"—but Schumpeter provides the most thorough analysis of this driving force.

As Robert Heilbroner writes in *The Worldly Philosophers*, Schumpeter was "the most romantic of economists. . . . Capitalism to his eyes had all the glamour and excitement of a knightly jousting tourney." Schumpeter spoke of the entrepreneur as an exceptional man of exceptional ability, who ventures out into the world of business with "the dream and the will to found a private kingdom, . . . the will to conquer, the impulse to fight, to prove oneself superior to others, to succeed for the sake, not of the fruits of success, but of success itself." The entrepreneur is motivated by "the joy of creating, of getting things done, or simply of exercising one's energy and ingenuity."

Schumpeter's second major work, the prodigious two-volume *Business Cycles* (1939), was intended as an elaboration of the central idea of his earlier work, an attempt to clothe the theory of innovation in statistical and historical fact. It is worthy of notice that here Schumpeter viewed the Great Depression of the 1930s as yet another business cycle to fit into his grand schema of things—and not as a unique, extraordinary break with historical experience. It is a subtle and an interesting twist that Schumpeter's sociological predictions, of which he appeared to be vaguely ashamed, survive, but Schumpeterian economics does not.

Marx versus Schumpeter

"Can capitalism survive?" Schumpeter asks. His answer: "No, I do not think it can." A century after Marx, and more than twenty-five years since Schumpeter's last thoughts on the matter, it is striking how wrong Marx is, and how right Schumpeter, on this issue. The standard Marxist vision of the class struggle and a violent overthrow of the capitalists due to the *failure* of

Joseph A. Schumpeter Revisited

the economic system has not been realized, but Schumpeter's prophecies concerning capitalism appear to be well on their way to being fulfilled. Nevertheless, as Clemence and Doody said some time ago in *The Schumpeterian System* (1950): "In recent years the Schumpeterian System has been the object of interest amounting nearly to apathy." This statement is even more true today in 1975. Yet the number of Marxists seems to be growing at least as rapidly as the relevance of Marx's analysis diminishes. [Still true in Western academe, says the author in 1994—*Ed.*]

In Schumpeter's "March into Socialism" address and at greater length in *Capitalism, Socialism, and Democracy* (1942), he argues that the success of capitalism leads to political and sociological changes that destroy the system. Put briefly, the capitalist class needs a precapitalist social milieu in order to flourish. As long as the affairs of church and state are taken care of by the nobility (the "protective strata" in Schumpeter's phrase), the entrepreneur will be able to succeed. Not only are social and political matters taken care of by someone else, but the very existence of such social distinctions—of both social and economic inequality—provides a driving force for the entrepreneur. Thus, the exceptional man of unexceptional birth, the typical entrepreneur, seeks to compete with the power of church and state, to substitute merit and rationality for tradition and authority as decision-making principles.

Capitalism needs to insist on equality before the law, and equality before supply and demand as well, in order to develop and grow. The successful business firm, the "private kingdom" of the entrepreneur, provides the innovator with recognition and status even in his own lifetime; his purchase of a baronial estate (suburban Connecticut?) and the establishment of a dynasty can extend such recognition even beyond it.

The capitalist class has succeeded beyond its wildest dreams, says Schumpeter. The profit motive has unleashed continuous and rapid technological progress, as one innovation calls forth countless others and the beauty of compound interest takes over. Capitalist progress has not been even or steady, of course; as innovations become imitated and absorbed in the economy,

George J. Viksnins

the profit margin shrinks and there is a temporary slowing of the growth rate. Business cycles of varying durations are superimposed upon each other, but the economic success of capitalism as a long-run phenomenon improves everyone's well-being tremendously.

This is a key point—the economic progress of capitalism leads to a very great absolute improvement in the standard of living for the masses. The lot of the upper 1 percent of the population has always been quite tolerable. It is the other 99 per cent that capitalism benefits.

Yet, the economic success of capitalism sows the seeds of its own destruction. The main arguments Schumpeter advanced for this hypothesis are sociological. First, he points to an inevitable "obsolescence of the entrepreneurial function." Large business firms grow ever larger—the corporation evolves from the family firm—and innovation becomes a matter of routine. The research departments of DuPont and Mitsubishi take care of the technical aspects of innovation, and their marketing and cost accounting staffs are responsible for the rest.

A new standard of living for all classes makes the economic function of the business class obsolescent and "amenable to bureaucratization." A few modern knights still sally forth on their own to found this computer service facility or that economic consulting firm, but society can do without them—and such individual efforts are viewed with deep suspicion by both big business and big government.

Class Unconscious

Schumpeter's second major argument is equally interesting. Capitalism goes hand in hand with representative governments and democracy. While these changes in the political system enable capitalism to function, free from the capricious interference of church and state, they also eventually lead to what Schumpeter terms the "destruction of the protective strata," the caretakers of the affairs of church and state—the nobility or upper classes.

Where is European nobility today? Working as waiters in New York, or jetting from Nice to Bangkok, depending on the skill

Joseph A. Schumpeter Revisited

or luck of their lawyers and accountants, but certainly not tending to the affairs of state. What of the Eastern Establishment in the United States? The affairs of state are left to parvenus from Texas and California, or even former football players from Ann Arbor. The care and feeding of American culture and education is often left to minority group members, and the hold of the Establishment is diminished even in the world of business and finance.

The abdication and elimination of the protective strata of the upper class forces the prospective entrepreneur to look after matters of church and state—giving speeches to the Kiwanis, serving on foreign policy councils and presidential commissions, and filling out endless governmental forms. This saps his energy and destroys his profit-maximizing soul.

A third powerful force is at work as well. The capitalistic process requires rationality in decision making—the calculus of revenue and cost, of profit and loss, extends itself into all areas of life. Schumpeter suggests that this rationality "turns upon itself"—destroying old loyalties and "habits of super- and subordination." Such habits, or class relationships if you will, are "essential for the efficient working of the institutionalized leadership of the producing plant." Worker loyalty, and a certain "fear of the boss" as well, is very much a thing of the past, as workers accumulate assets (including investment in the education of the next generation as an important part of the portfolio), union seniority, and unemployment benefit rights.

Akin to this force is a fourth Schumpeterian argument concerning the role of intellectuals as a separate class. Capitalist rationality at first encourages an attitude of independence on the part of the educational establishment and its intellectuals, scientific inquiry being an important component of innovation. However, as rationality spreads from the physical sciences and their derivative fields to politics and social relationships (the sociology of religion, for example), the assumptions and structure of capitalism itself come into question. As Robert Heilbroner says: "Daring as the capitalist was, his civilization was built on a rational, inquiring, skeptical attitude. Originally that rationalism had destroyed the pretensions of kings and lords. But now it turned its cold and disconcerting gaze on itself. 'Money isn't everything,' said the intellectuals, and in so doing they sowed a seed of doubt about the values of money-making as an end in itself."

This seed of doubt has sprouted, flowered, and brought forth its fruit. "Free enterprise" and "capitalism" are by now dirty words, and the independence of the intellectuals of an earlier era has somehow turned into a hostility to capitalism, as Schumpeter foresaw. "Profit" has become "ripoff"—and most of the economists quoted in the media appear to be ready to trade in the allocative properties of the old ripoff system for something better.

The Liberal's Checklist

While this something better would not necessarily be called centralist socialism, since Americans are very sensitive to words, most economists would certainly favor greater "security, equality, and regulation." The following is Schumpeter's checklist for the orthodox liberal economist. Do you believe in:
1. Stabilization policies aimed at full or high employment? Of course.
2. The desirability of a greater equality of incomes? Fervently.
3. Regulation of prices, particularly in highly concentrated industries? Probably.
4. Public control over the labor and money markets? We work at the FRB, FDIC, NLRB, SEC, Fannie-Ginnie-Freddie Mae, BLS, and the like.
5. Extension of the sphere of public wants? Indubitably.
6. Better social security legislation? Yes, indeed.

Since Schumpeter wrote, the strength of the trend in favor of socialization has increased, of course. It is true that there is an ebb and flow to this process, as Schumpeter also foresaw. Controls are tried for a time, repealed, and then tried again. But ultimately, as Schumpeter predicted, "The remedy for unsuccessful socialization which will suggest itself will not be less but more socialization." The regulation of the railroads has turned into quasi-public ownership, and taxpayers are increas-

Joseph A. Schumpeter Revisited

ingly forced to support organizations that they refuse to support as consumers.

The transformation of social orders is incessant but slow, says Schumpeter, though it can be accelerated by wars and by inflation. His analysis of inflation is particularly relevant today: "Irresponsible revolutionaries alone excepted," everyone else should consider inflation Public Enemy No. 1. It is the very existence of inflation, moreover, and not so much its quantitative magnitude, that is important: "A state of perennial inflationary pressure will have, qualitatively, all the effects of weakening the social framework of society and of strengthening subversive tendencies... that every competent economist is in the habit of attributing to [the] more spectacular inflations."

Furthermore, Schumpeter questioned the efficacy of monetary and fiscal policy in preventing further increases in the price level. Higher interest rates "achieve little beyond increasing the difficulties of business," since any real impact on employment and output would "immediately provoke government action to neutralize them." The speed with which nearly everyone moved from advocating higher taxes to favoring a tax cut in 1974–75 is a good object lesson on this point. Moreover, says Schumpeter, higher taxes that affect saving and investment may reduce aggregate demand in the short run, but are probably inflationary in the long run because of their effects on the supply side. Thus, we are left with direct controls.

Schumpeter viewed controls as a means of cutting off the last line of retreat for business. They are "a surrender of private enterprise to public authority," a "big stride toward the perfectly planned economy." To be sure, some fringe areas of private decision making may remain. Schumpeter spoke of the "subsidized independence of the farmer" as being politically very sensitive; certain small business activities, akin to the private plots in the *kolkhoz*, are probably too strong "for bureaucracy to conquer." An analogy to the army seems apt—individual unit commanders do have some decision-making power, but as to whether and when the colossus moves, the decision comes from above.

George J. Viksnins

No doubt the housewife will continue to be able to choose between Cheer and Tide, and the college student between majoring in French and Spanish, but capitalism as a system, as an historical experiment, will be gone. This was Schumpeter's basic message, an unheeded warning, some would say: Capitalism, the civilization of inequality and family fortune, is rapidly passing away. As Schumpeter said, "Let us rejoice or else lament the fact as much as every one of us likes; but do not let us shut our eyes to it."

A Postscript For 1994

In the preface of the second edition of his book, Schumpeter softened his pessimism about the future of capitalism a bit. If they are told that the ship is sinking, he wrote, the crew can sit on the deck and get drunk—or they can get buckets and start bailing. In recent years, several volumes about Schumpeter have appeared, including one in 1981, *Schumpeter's Vision: Capitalism, Socialism and Democracy after 40 Years*, edited by Arnold Heertje, which contains thoughtful essays by a number of prominent economists. Robert Heibroner in his essay "Was Schumpeter right?" answers, "No, I do not think he was."

In the 1970s, the world did not even guess the extent to which socialism in practice had failed dismally. While growth rates in the Comecon countries had been coming down, they were still quite respectable, and specialists in the comparative systems field were still debating quite seriously whether living conditions on the other side of the Berlin Wall were significantly worse. To be sure, the Trabant was not a Mercedes, but the collapse of the system seemed unlikely. Environmental disasters, endemic shortages, revolt in the satellites, and the widening technological gap were still in the future back then. It was quite fashionable to be in favor of democratic socialism, despite warnings by Hayek and Friedman that those two words are fundamentally incompatible. In academia, radicals were gaining tenure, and support of capitalism was becoming politically incorrect.

Joseph A. Schumpeter Revisited

Central planning requires terror. As Mancur Olson has written, Stalin had an "all-encompassing interest" in the economic success of the Soviet Union, indeed, of the entire socialist system. Such success was defined in terms of achieving (and overachieving) planned growth rates, rapidly rising industrial output (especially steel and machinery), and a growing defense/aerospace/research establishment. Positive indicators in these areas enhanced Stalin's personal prestige and the international stature of the system, and any negative developments could be "swept under the rug." Anyone showing a morbid interest in such negatives—or perhaps even just reporting them—could be shipped off to the Gulags. Money and foreign trade did not matter under the classical socialist system; households used cash, but enterprises could only use Gosbank balances to make payments approved by the Gosplan. Exports and imports were also under centralized control.

This system began to unravel slowly after Stalin's death, and "distributional coalitions" (Olson's concept) began to gain in importance. Estonian and Latvian planners had a mildly positive interest in all-Union performance, but were much more interested in budgetary allocations, capital investments, and imports coming into their territory. As money and foreign trade became decentralized, the unraveling of the classical system accelerated greatly.

By now, it has become obvious that even those countries still willing to use terror to enforce central planning directives, such as China or North Korea, are beginning to question the wisdom of continuing with a Stalinist model. The theoretical appeal of any socialist model has been greatly mitigated by its evident failure in practice. While Marxism continues to be taught in elite Western universities, the transition economies look more to Milton Friedman.

In the West, the trend toward greater state involvement in economic life was substantially slowed by two remarkable personalities, Ronald Reagan and Margaret Thatcher, and their supply-side policies. Cuts in tax rates and indexation of exemptions in the United States successfully slowed the growth in government revenues, but the ratio of government spending to national income continued to drift upward. That upward drift accelerated under George Bush, and seems likely to rise a bit more under Bill Clinton.

Thus, Schumpeter's basic message—we are drifting toward government control of most economic decisions—is probably still valid. Granted, inflation has been reduced remarkably, which is a very hopeful sign. For Schumpeter, nevertheless, governmental control over wages and prices appears to be the determining act in curtailing finally the freedom of action of the entrepreneur. Though that does not seem to loom just around the corner in 1994, what about 2004? Or 2014?

CHAPTER 10

Scholarship on the Laws of War: Some Reflections

WILLIAM V. O'BRIEN

Bill O'Brien's internationally recognized scholarship was unique in combining legal, moral, and military dimensions in the study of just war theory. His courses consistently ranked among the most popular at Georgetown, where he taught international law and relations (with emphasis on legal and moral issues of war) from 1950 to 1993. He chaired the committee that invented the undergraduate core curriculum of the School of Foreign Service and twice chaired the government department. Faculty colleagues and former students honored him upon his retirement by establishing a biennial William V. O'Brien Lecture in International Law and Morality. What follows is the inaugual lecture in the series, delivered by Professor O'Brien himself on April 16, 1993.

Scholarship on the Laws of War: Some Reflections

These reflections on a liftetime of research and writing on the laws of war concern both the international law of war and contemporary just war doctrine. These legal and moral sources of normative restraint on war are in turn divided into two parts: the legality and morality of recourse to armed force—traditionally the *jus ad bellum*, which I call war-decision law—and the legality and morality of conduct in war—traditionally the *jus in bello*, which I call war-conduct law.

These reflections do not purport to be a comprehensive survey of the literature and ongoing scholarship in these fields. They are limited to my personal experience as a scholar, begun as a graduate student under the tutelage of Ernst H. Feilchenfeld.[1] Returning from three years in the Army of the United States during World War II, I was to pursue my studies in the environment of the Cold War and the Korean War. Henceforth, during most of my years as a teacher and scholar I was a civil affairs officer in the Army's Ready Reserve.

My academic career has covered the development of the nuclear balance of terror and multiple revolutionary or counterinsurgency wars and interventions therein. These include the Vietnam War, the wars of the Arab-Israeli conflict, in which I have had a particular interest, U.S. military interventions in Latin America, the emergence of threats to the peace from Iran and Iraq, Desert Shield and Desert Storm, and, most recently, efforts at collective humanitarian intervention in Somalia and the former Yugoslavia.

Although the Cold War has been declared over, the future of Russia and other parts of the Soviet Union remains in question, as does the future of huge arsenals of nuclear, chemical, and biological weapons and long-range delivery systems in the

William V. O'Brien

former Soviet Union, China, and other parts of Asia and the Middle East. Evidence of intractable, colliding nationalist and ethnic aspirations, fueled by hatred and demands for vengeance, increase just as we sigh with relief at the end of the Cold War. I would happily concede to my successors that, while preoccupation with security issues and the laws of war was appropriate to my liftetime as a scholar, the next generation of scholars in the fields of international law and morality might better pursue more positive subjects related to legal and moral issues of peace, cooperation, and justice, relegating the laws of war to a secondary position. Unfortunately, current trends do not encourage such a concession.

While scholarship and teaching in the law of peace should continue its expansion from a law dominated by the need for order in international relations to a law increasingly concerned with cooperation and justice, the laws of war remain a major necessity in these times. Some of the sources of conflict have changed, but their violent and disruptive effects on the international system have in many ways increased the need for realistic legal and moral approaches to the perennial dilemmas of war.

The central motif of these reflections is the continuing gap between the scholarship of international lawyers and moralists, on one hand, and the scholarship and practical work of practitioners in international relations and military science on the other. The challenge of the future is to narrow this gap.

I will discuss this challenge in terms of the possibilities for improved scholarship in three related areas: (1) the need for better understanding of practical problems of international conflict through greater recourse by legal and moral scholars to the literature of international relations, security studies, and military history and science in order to compare legal and moral prescriptions with the actual practice and expectations of belligerents; (2) the need for improved understanding of the role of legal and moral guidelines in the processes of security decision making and the implemenation of security policies; and (3) recognition of the advantages of increasing recourse to modern just war doctrine as a normative complement—and

Scholarship on the Laws of War: Some Reflections

sometimes alternative—to international war-decision and war-conduct law.

INCREASING LEGAL AND MORAL SCHOLARS' USE OF THE LITERATURE ON INTERNATIONAL ARMED CONFLICT

The importance of legal and moral guidelines for the use of armed force has been increasingly recognized. Scholarship on this subject, however, still falls short of what is required to improve the laws of war to make them more normatively compelling and, at the same time, more realistic.

Legal and moral prescriptions regarding the use of armed force in international conflicts, as well as in revolutionary/counterinsurgency wars, are seldom enforced by international organizations or even by considerations of reciprocity or fear of reprisals. Such prescriptions should be normatively compelling and realistic if they are to be taken seriously by belligerents committed to legal and moral standards of behavior—such as the United States. It should be the task of scholarship in the laws of war to make the best normative arguments for putative legal and moral prescriptions, based on the best analyses of the practical political, military, and other empirical considerations that must be recognized if these prescriptions are to be realistic.

The task of legal and moral analyses of international conflict—indeed of most international interaction, peaceful as well as belligerent—has been rendered more difficult by the inadequate relationship between scholarship in international law and morality and scholarship in the fields of international relations, security studies, and military history and science. Any normative study should begin with a reasonable understanding of the material "stuff" of the subject matter. Yet any sampling of the literature on the laws of war will reveal that much of it rests largely on legal and moral sources—lawyers and moralists citing lawyers and moralists, with insufficient references to the literature on wars, their causes, their conduct, their consequences, in short, the contexts in which legal and moral issues arise.

William V. O'Brien

In 1963, for example, when studies of international conflict by international relations scholars abounded, a leading British international law scholar, Ian Brownlie, in his *International Law and the Use of Force by States,* supported his analyses of international war-decision law entirely by citing international conventions, often honored in the breach, such as the Kellog-Briand Pact, and the opinions of other legal scholars.[2] Louis Henkin, who ranks among the foremost American international law scholars, has published two editions of a book entitled *How Nations Behave.*[3] Reflecting little of the realities of contemporary international conflict, it might better have been entitled "How Nations Ought to Behave According to Henkin." Comparable examples could be cited from the writings of moralists, even those who accept some form of just war doctrine.[4]

These examples concern the law on recourse to armed force, the *jus ad bellum* or war-decision law. There is little serious literature on the *jus in bello,* war-conduct law. What there is suffers from insufficient reference to a number of bodies of literature, including that on nuclear deterrence and defense, limited war, revolutionary war/counterinsurgency, and terrorism-counterterrorism.

In particular there is scant reference to contemporary military history. After World War I, there were books on the record of observance of the laws of war in that conflict.[5] Indeed, the Japanese government commissioned a Japanese international law scholar to observe conduct in the Russo-Japanese War of 1904–1905 and produce a book on the laws of war in that conflict.[6] To the best of my knowledge there is no work on the laws of war in World War II or the Korean War. Guenter Lewy's *America in Vietnam*[7] deals in authoritative detail with key war-conduct law issues in the Vietnam War, but there is no comprehensive work on international law in that conflict.[8]

Criticism of the lack of recourse to empirical studies of contemporary armed conflict by international law scholars and moralists is not new. Already in the 1950s and 1960s, Harold Lasswell and Myres S. McDougal were insisting on scholars' need to make informed, sophisticated analyses of what they called the "process of interaction." Such analyses were to be

Scholarship on the Laws of War: Some Reflections

made before undertaking normative analyses—in the "process of claims"—of justifications advanced for state actions, and before making final determination—in the "process of authoritative decision"—of what is legally permissible. Lasswell, McDougal, and their collaborators drew heavily on the literature of international relations, security studies, and military history and science in their comprehensive discussions of contemporary problems of armed conflict.[9] This emphasis on coordinating empirical with normative analyses has been continued by some of McDougal's successors, notably John Norton Moore and W. Michael Reisman.[10]

International Law in International Relations Studies. The gap between international law generally, the laws of war in particular, and international relations studies is reflected in contemporary academic programs. International law is not a "bread-and-butter" bar exam subject in most law schools. Law school courses in international law tend toward practical professional subjects, such as international ecnomic or commercial law, conflicts of law, or perhaps environmental law. The closest that most law school courses come to the laws of war is through the study of international human rights law, which seldom embraces the serious military considerations that ought to inform the laws of war. Generally speaking, law schools are not the likely locus for studies of laws of war.

More logically, graduate programs in international relations might be the home of laws-of-war studies, since international conflict is obviously a central concern and such programs have been informed by the enormous growth of security studies. Unfortunately, this has not been the case.

International law generally has not prospered in contemporary international relations programs. A recent study of the place of international law in such programs by Charlotte Ku and John King Gamble concludes:

> In less than one academic generation, at many institutions, international law retrogressed from mainstream to periphery to oblivion. Evidence of this deterioration is inescapable.

William V. O'Brien

> Those teaching international law in departments of political science tend to be senior people, often semi-retired, who may not be replaced when they stop teaching. Many of the largest and most distinguished departments of political science (or government) offer no international law whatever and feel none the worse for it.[11]

Ku and Gamble suggest five reasons for the decline of international law in international relations programs:

1. International law has been "perceived as unable or at least unwilling" to employ the quantitative techniques and methods developed in political science since the 1960s.
2. International law is too normative for scholars whose interest is largely confined to the supposedly scientific description of behavior.
3. International law is "too wedded to the status quo" for scholars brought up to promote change.
4. International law is too narrowly focused on marginal subjects.
5. International law is irrelevant to the real world, where state action is not guided by legal considerations.[12]

International law scholars and their colleagues among the moralists need not apologize for not using some social science methods and techniques not relevant to their work. They certainly can protest the avoidance or rejection of normative issues in politics, whether international or domestic. From earliest times scholars have sought to discover the "ought" as well as the "is" in human behavior. The issue of orientation toward status quo rather than change can hardly be resolved by generalizations. Either can be good, bad, or indifferent depending on specific cases. However, it should be recognized that the last two reasons suggested by Ku and Gamble for the decline of international law as a discipline ought to be considered seriously by international law scholars.

Certainly much international law scholarship tends to be narrow and technical, of little interest to those concerned with

Scholarship on the Laws of War: Some Reflections

high politics. Moreover, too narrow a focus on so-called "black letter law" (that is, literal, legalistic interpretations of law) can incline the would-be realists of international relations studies to ignore or even ridicule international legal and moral scholarship. Ironically, if such scholarship could be extended beyond exercises in textual analyses and interpretations of the United Nations Charter, international conventions, the decisions of the International Court of Justice and other international tribunals, and formal governmental pronouncements, it might be demonstrated to the sceptics that international legal and moral issues play a greater part in international relations than is generally recognized.

INTERNATIONAL LAW AND MORALITY IN FOREIGN AND DEFENSE POLICY DECISION PROCESSES

Historically, evidence of "state practice" with respect to international law has been deduced mainly from the language of international agreements and formal state policy statements. It is not sufficient merely to accept their provisions at face value as evidence of serious observance and implementation. Such documents may range from truthful statements of policy to vague assurances of good behavior, not always validated in practice, to simple fraudulent propaganda. Accordingly, correction of unjustified versions of a state's observance of international law requires comparison of its behavior with its declaratory postures. As already suggested, this may be accomplished with the help of international relations scholars by studying the record of state interaction.

Another way is to probe into the policy processes of governments as they deal with foreign and defense issues. Traditionally, this approach has been problematic. Governments have usually been reluctant to open up their archives to external scrutiny until long after the events therein recorded. The international legal and moral implications of old archives are valuable, but they may not offer much insight into contemporary practice. However, the possibilities of obtaining access to current evidence of state practice, especially to current and recent decision makers and advisers, appear to be increasing.

WILLIAM V. O'BRIEN

One source of information and insights about policy processes is the work of investigative journalists. Journalists such as Bob Woodward in books like *The Commanders*[13] present a version of the foreign and defense policy processes acquired by a variety of techniques. These include imaginative use of Freedom of Information laws and straightforward interviews with present or recent participants in policy processes. They may also include use of leaks and purloined documents.

Journalistic accounts of this kind may sometimes contain information relevant to the role of international law and morality in a particular policy process. My impression, however, is that there is not usually much concern with normative issues unless there are prospects for revealing reprehensible and/or illegal conduct. What is needed are scholarly inquiries, also with current and recent participants in foreign and defense policy processes who may be willing, preferably on the record, to discuss the way that international legal and moral issues are raised, discussed, and resolved.

I am familar with one such effort, in particular, regarding the role of war-decision law. I was mentor of a now-published Ph.D. dissertation by Robert Beck on the role of international law in the decision processes preceding the 1983 intervention in Grenada.[14] Beck was able to obtain candid interviews with officials who had participated in the decision to intervene in Grenada and to compare the Reagan administration's declaratory positions on the legality of the intervention with the actual role of legal and moral norms in the decision process.

International relations scholars have long been probing foreign and defense policy processes, but there has been little attempt to focus this kind of scholarship on issues of law and morality.[15] Beck has provided a model for scholarship that may penetrate the world of what Myres McDougal has called "authoritative decision-makers," greatly enhancing our ability to report and assess the practice and expectations of states.[16]

In addition to studies of law and morality in policy processes by outside scholars, there are also possibilities for such studies to be made and published by persons within the government. An outstanding example of international legal scholarship is

Scholarship on the Laws of War: Some Reflections

found in the works of W. Hays Parks. Parks may well be the best qualified and most productive war-conduct scholar writing today. He was both a tactical combat commander and a military lawyer as a young Marine officer in Vietnam, served as an active duty Marine JAG officer, and then took over a civilian position in the Department of the Army as chief of the International Law Branch, International Affairs Division, in the Office of the Judge Advocate General. Meanwhile Parks continued to be active in the Marine Reserve until retiring as a colonel. Hays Parks knows the weapons and means of modern warfare. He knows the decision processes that produce military strategies, tactics, and policies. He has participated in the decisions leading to contemporary cases of recourse to armed force by the United States. In addition, he is a military scholar who has produced major contributions to the literature on war-conduct law.[17]

One of the reasons for his success is that he has been able to convince Pentagon officials that it is better to provide the best, most authoritative and candid version of U.S. military actions— such as the 1972 "Christmas bombing" campaign against Hanoi, excoriated at the time as a war crime,[18] and the 1986 U.S. bombing of terrorist bases in Libya—than to bury the record in classified files. The U.S. Armed Forces often carry out their missions with much greater fidelity to the laws of war than they are given credit for. This was certainly the case in Vietnam. If the U.S. government had been more forthcoming with evidence of concern for observance of the laws of war while admitting cases of violations, the field might not have been left to critics able to establish a perception of generalized lawlessness and immorality, perpetuated by Hollywood.

THE ROLE OF JUST WAR DOCTRINE

Just war doctrine has a long history both as an independent source of normative guidance and as a companion to the positive international law of war. This history has been admirably traced and explained by James Turner Johnson.[19] Much of just war *jus in bello* comes from the practice of belligerents, notably in the Age of Chivalry and in the period of limited European

WILLIAM V. O'BRIEN

wars from 1648 to 1789. The contemporary international war-decison law, *jus ad bellum*, tends to be incorporated into just war *jus ad bellum*. But there are important differences between the international laws of war and just war doctrine.

International war-decision law consists of limited categories whose application depends on judgment calls. It begins with Article 2 (4) of the UN Charter, which prohibits "the threat or use of force against the territorial integrity or political independence of any state, or in any other manner inconsistent with the purposes of the United Nations." This clearly prohibits unprovoked attacks with conventional forces across established international boundaries, such as Hitler's 1939 invasion of Poland or Saddam Hussein's 1990 invasion of Kuwait. In the contemporary era, however, the threat or use of force usually does not take the form of clear conventional aggression. More often it is the continuing threat and/or use of indirect aggression through exported revolution and other forms of intervention in civil strife, frequently taking the form of state-sponsored or state-supported terrorism and subversion.

Efforts to define "aggression," that is, violation of Article 2 (4), have not been successful. The definition of aggression has been left, in the first instance, to the UN Security Council. In effect, what the Security Council determines to be aggression is aggression. If the Security Council can agree that aggression is imminent and/or in progress, that there is a "threat to the peace," it can order "enforcement action" under Articles 41 and 42 of the Charter. This has only occurred once, in the 1990–91 Gulf War.[20]

Unfortunately, the Security Council has not operated as envisaged by the Charter until very recently, as the collapse of the Soviet Union led to a more effective Council. Still, this development depends on the continued cooperation of the United States and Russia, on China, and on the various dispositions of the other permanent and nonpermanent members.

Moreover, Article 2 (4) rests on the basic assumption of the Charter that all sovereign states are equal and that any threat or use of force not justified as individual or collective self-defense—an "inherent" right reiterated in Article 51 of the UN

Scholarship on the Laws of War: Some Reflections

Charter—is a violation of the UN system, wherein war-avoidance is the highest value. However, there appears to be an increasing reluctance to accept such an assumption. More and more practitioners and scholars hold that, in certain cases, justice, as they define it, is a higher value than war-avoidance. This is especially true of elites in states and movements with revolutionary ideologies that seek to overthrow the status quo, but also of state and movement elites committed to fundamental human rights, which they find some states violating to a genocidal extent. Iran and Libya do not accept the status quo, do not really accept the UN Charter and its war-decision law, and clearly place the achievement of justice as they define it above any norm of war-avoidance. Moreover, in pursuit of what are, in effect, holy wars, they deny the limitations of war-conduct law and, indeed, specialize in the promotion of indiscriminate terrorism.

Most international law scholars and moralists would reject the claims of such forms of holy war. Increasingly, however, there is evidence of a desire to bring justice to at least parity with war-avoidance as a basic value in the international system.[21] The rise of genocidal practices in Cambodia, Uganda, Iraq, and now former Yugoslavia seems to have pushed more and more international law scholars and moralists, however hesitantly, to the realization that it is not enough to bar use of force against any or all sovereign states on the basis of sovereign equality.

While it is obviously a subjective and potentially divisive exercise to distinguish good and tolerable states from evil states, it is incontestable that there are evil states in the world, that such states are engaged in evil practices to an intolerable extent, and that some provision must be made for the suppression of those practices and, if necessary, of the regimes in evil states. This realization is emerging in the concept of humanitarian intervention.

The principle of nonintervention, based on the sovereign equality of states, has long been proclaimed in international law and diplomacy—albeit frequently violated.[22] Historically, four possible exceptions to the principle of nonintervention

William V. O'Brien

have been advanced to justify military intervention:
1. Intervention by treaty right and duty, such as the United States in Panama.
2. Intervention by invitation, usually claimed as counterintervention against antecedent intervention hostile to the host state.
3. Intervention to protect a state's nationals and those of other countries threatened by clear and present danger in time of internal conflict or collapse of authority.
4. Humanitarian intervention to protect a foreign people from extreme violations of their human rights by their own government.[23]

In assessing the permissibility of intervention under any of these justifications it is necessary to evaluate the "reasonableness" of the intervention. Just war doctrine can be extremely useful, since it requires conditions for recourse to armed force that go beyond a plausible case that it is "legal" or "illegal." The *jus ad bellum*, war-decision law of just war doctrine requires that a belligerent have *competent authority*, a *just cause, comparative justice, probability of success, proportionality of means to just end, reasonable exhaustion of peaceful alternatives*, and *right intention*.[24] A just belligerent must also observe the *jus in bello*, war-conduct principles of proportion and discrimination as well as the positive laws of war.[25]

International law scholars and practitioners sometimes tend to view just war doctrine with skepticism, fearing that it offers rationales for escaping the supposed rigors of the positive international law of war. Such fears are well grounded with respect to holy war doctrines that hold, in effect, that just ends justify any means; but they are not warranted with respect to just war doctrine. On the contrary, just war doctrine responsibly applied is more demanding in its requirements than the positive international law of war.

Consider the most prominent form of military intervention debated in 1993, humanitarian intervention, and the main contingency contemplated, humanitarian intervention in former Yugoslavia. It is conceivable that a NATO force might be authorized by the UN Security Council, under Article 42, to in-

Scholarship on the Laws of War: Some Reflections

tervene in Bosnia and other new entities in former Yugoslavia to put a stop to continuing Serbian aggression and violations of human rights that may properly be condemned as genocide. Under the UN Charter's war-decision legal regime, such a UN enforcement action would clearly be legally permissible. Alternatively, NATO forces or those of some other coalition might intervene under Article 51 under the right of collective self-defense.

To be sure, authorization of UN enforcement action might be difficult to obtain in the Security Council, but it would be a clear case of legally permissible use of armed force. Given the notorious factual situation in former Yugoslavia, even a coalition intervention not authorized by the Security Council would have a strong case based on collective self-defense and humanitarian intervention to stop genocidal behavior.

Just war doctrine requires more than legal permissibility, however. The issue of competent authority would be raised in each state participating in the intervention in the form of the constitutional issue of power to commit the nation's armed forces to war. In the United States this would once again involve the relationship between the president's powers as commander-in-chief and the power of Congress to declare war.

On the face of it, there would be a clear just cause, namely, collective defense against aggression and suppression of genocidal behavior. Likewise, given the character of the regimes in Serbia and the emerging Serbian entities in Croatia, Bosnia, and possibly other parts of former Yugoslavia, there is a clear case of comparative justice on the side of the victims of Serbian aggression and "ethnic cleansing." There is thus an equally clear case for considering intervention in former Yugoslavia as a potentially just war.

But just war doctrine does not stop at the requirements for competent authority, just cause, and comparative justice. In its central core, just war doctrine requires that the probable good to result from achievement of the just cause be proportionate to the damage done by the necessary means, viewed in the light of the probability of success. Moreover, just war doctrine requires that the estimate of probability of success be made not only at the outset but continually through a conflict. What appeared to be feasible at a proportionate price may later prove to be impossible to achieve at a proportionate price—or at any price. At this point, no matter how just and desirable the cause, the just belligerent must seek some way out of the war.

It is precisely considerations of this kind that appear to have discouraged intervention in the Yugoslav conflict. Just war doctrine can help order the consideration of and debates on possible intervention. Meanwhile, just war doctrine requires reasonable efforts to find peaceful alternatives to recourse to armed force. Here again, just war doctrine calls for conscientious efforts to avoid war; just war scholars often label this condition *last resort*.[26]

I find this an unfortunate label. Too literal an interpretation of last resort may encourage Munichs. In the present case of disintegrating Yugoslavia, literal application of the last resort requirement may well mean that aggression and "ethnic cleansing" have gone so far that there is no just cause left to defend.

Finally, the war-decision law of just war doctrine requires right intention. This means that the just belligerent must limit its pursuit of the just war to the achievement of the just cause and not expand the conflict beyond that; it must not fight in a spirit of hatred and vengeance; and it must make every effort to ensure that the conduct of the war maximizes the chances for a just and lasting peace.

These conditions are manifestly hard to meet, especially in a case such as that of intervention in former Yugoslavia, where the outrageous conduct of the Serbs has contributed to a cycle of violence and hatred going back centuries. Nevertheless, right intention is necessary for a just belligerent, and it is also necessary in political-military terms for a controlled use of the military instrument.

Clearly the war-decision requirements of just war doctrine raise difficult issues that must be dealt with if recourse to armed force, even for a manifestly just cause, is to be justified. Moreover, further requirements are set forth in war-conduct law, most fundamentally the requirements of proportion and discrimination. Proportion in war-conduct law means the proportion of

Scholarship on the Laws of War: Some Reflections

military measures at the strategic and tactical levels, not the grand strategic proportion of ends and means required in war-decision law. A key aspect of the principle of proportion is that judgments of military necessity at the strategic and tactical levels must not conflict with the requirements of grand strategic proportionality. Actions by tactical battlefield commanders, for example, that appear to be reasonable in the tactical context may conflict with the overall requirement of grand strategic proportion. This is particularly true of decisions concerning use of modern firepower. Multiplication of instances where excessive firepower is employed may be understandable from the standpoint of tactical commanders but may conflict with the overall grand strategic goal of keeping the means proportionate to the just end.

Likewise, the firepower and mobility of modern armed forces and the location of so many of the world's battle zones in places having both large concentrations of noncombatants and civilian targets and military forces and targets makes it difficult to observe the principle of discrimination—that is, noncombatant immunity from direct intentional attack. Nevertheless, the just belligerent must maximize efforts to avoid disproportionate civilian damage.

This means that before deciding to launch a just military intervention in a conflict such as that raging in former Yugoslavia, responsible decision makers must envisage realistically what kind of war will be waged and the extent to which the just belligerents will be able to respect the principles of proportion and discrimination. As contingency plans are developed for such an intervention, there must be conscientious efforts to ensure that strategies, tactics, selection of weapons systems to be employed, training, rules of engagement, and provisions for control of operations within the chain of command maximize the degree to which the war will be fought in consonance with the principles of proportion and discrimination.

Clearly just war scholars as well as international law scholars must have the benefit of the expertise of military scholars and practitioners in assessing the prospects for possible just interventions and the record of ongoing or completed interventions.

WILLIAM V. O'BRIEN

In my own research on Israel's war with the PLO, I found a sharp contrast between the evaluations of Israeli conduct in the 1982 Lebanon War by journalists and legal and moral scholars, on one hand, and by military historians and analysts on the other.[27]

In summary, just war doctrine does not supply answers; it poses questions that must be answered persuasively before judging a belligerent to be waging a just war. It includes the war-decision and war-conduct law of international law but goes far beyond them in a comprehensive normative framework. Accordingly, just war doctrine offers decision makers, private persons, and the general public indispensable normative guidance on the decision to go to war and the manner of its conduct. However, as in any formulation of moral and legal guidance, the legal scholars and moralists must consult other relevant scholars and practitioners—in medicine, economic and social relations, international relations, and military history and science—if their guidance is to be realistic and compelling.

Scholarship on the Laws of War: Some Reflections

ENDNOTES

1. Ernst H. Feilchenfeld is the author of *Public Debts and State Succession* (New York: Macmillan, 1932); *The International Economic Law of Belligerent Occupation* (Washington, D.C.: Carnegie Endowment of International Peace, 1942); and *Prisoners of War* (Washington, D.C.: Institute of World Polity, School of Foreign Service, Georgetown University, 1948).

2. Ian Brownlie, *International Law and the Use of Force by States* (Oxford: Clarendon Press, 1963).

3. Louis Henkin, *How Nations Behave* (New York: Council on Foreign Relations/Columbia University Press, 1979).

4. See, for example, "Just-War Criteria," in *War or Peace? The Search for New Answers*, ed. Thomas A. Shannon (Maryknoll, N.Y.: Orbis, 1980), pp. 40–58.

5. See A. Merignhac and E. Lemonon, *Le droit des gens et la guerre de 1914–1918*, 2 vols. (Paris: Librairie Birey, 1921); and James Wilford Garner, *International Law and the World War*, 2 vols. (London: Longmans, Green, 1920).

6. Nagos Ariga, *La guerre Russo-Japonaise au point de vue continental et le droit international* (Paris: Pedone, 1908).

7. Guenter Lewy, *America in Vietnam* (New York: Oxford University Press, 1978).

8. Both war-decision and war-conduct issues are addressed in the collections edited by Richard A. Falk, *The Vietnam War in International Law* 4 vols. (Princeton, N.J.: Princeton University Press, 1969–76), but there is apparently no single volume written, as was Lewy's, with the benefit of records and analyses available after the war.

9. See, for example, Myres S. McDougal & Associates, *Studies in World Public Order* (New Haven, Conn.: Yale University Press, 1960); and Myres S. McDougal and Florentino P. Feliciano, *Law and Minimum World Public Order* (New Haven, Conn.: Yale University Press, 1962).

10. See, for example, John Norton Moore, *Law and Civil War in the Modern World* (Baltimore, Md.: Johns Hopkins University Press, 1974); and W. Michael Reisman and Andrew M. Willard, *International Incidents: The Law That Counts in International Politics* (Princeton, N.J.: Princeton University Press, 1988).

11. "International Law: 'State of the Discipline,'" *International Studies Notes* 16:3 (Fall 1991), and 17:1 (Winter 1992), p. 47.

12. Ibid., 17:1, pp. 47–48.

13. Bob Woodward, *The Commanders* (New York: Simon & Schuster, 1991).

14. Robert J. Beck, *The Grenada Invasion: Politics, Law and Foreign Policy* (Boulder, Col.: Westview, 1993).

15. See, for example, I.M. Destler, *Presidents, Bureaucrats and Foreign Policy* (Princeton, N.J.: Princeton University Press, 1974); and Charles W. Kegley, Jr., and Eugene R. Wittkopf, *American Foreign Policy: Pattern and Process* (New York: St. Martin's, 1979).

16. See, for example, Myres S. McDougal and Florentino P. Feliciano, "International Coercion and World Public Order: The General Principles of the Laws of War," in McDougal & Associates, *Studies in World Public Order*, pp. 275–76.

17. See, for example, these works by Major, then Colonel, William Hays Parks: "Command Responsibility for War Crimes," *Military Law Review* 62:1–104; "The

WILLIAM V. O'BRIEN

Law of War Adviser," *JAG Journal* 31 (Summer 1980):1–52; "Rolling Thunder and the Law of War," *Air University Review* 33 (January–February 1982):2–23; "Linebacker and the Law of War," *Air University Review* 34 (January–February 1983):2–30; "Crossing the Line," *U.S. Naval Institute Proceedings* 112 (November 1986):40–52.

18 See, for example, Henry A. Kissinger, *White House Years* (Boston, Little, Brown, 1979), pp. 1552–55.

19 James Turner Johnson, *Ideology, Reason and Limitation of War* (Princeton, N.J.: Princeton University Press, 1975); idem, *Just War Tradition and Restraint of War* (Princeton, N.J.: Princeton University Press, 1981); and idem, *Can Modern War Be Just?* (New Haven, Conn.: Yale University Press, 1984).

20 William V. O'Brien, *Law and Morality in Israel's War with the PLO* (New York: Routledge, 1991), pp. 88–90.

21 See Anthony Clark Arend and Robert J. Beck, *International Law and the Use of Force* (New York & London: Routledge, 1992), pp. 191–93.

22 See William V. O'Brien, *The Conduct of Just and Limited War* (New York: Praeger, 1981), pp. 167–74 and authorities cited therein.

23 Ibid., pp.170–73.

24 See Ibid., pp. 275–87.

25 Ibid.

26 James F. Childress employs the term "last resort" but qualifies it to mean the equivalent of reasonable exhaustion of peaceful alternatives ("Just-War Criteria," in Shannon, ed., *War or Peace*, p. 46). See James Turner Johnson's similar interpretation of last resort in *Can Modern War Be Just?* (New Haven, Conn.: Yale University Press, 1984), pp. 24–25, 147. Johnson criticizes the American Catholic Bishops' 1983 pastoral letter, *The Challenge of Peace* (Washington, D.C.: U.S. Catholic Conference, 1983), which, in his opinion and mine, pushes the concept of last resort so far as to constitute an overwhelming presumption against recourse to armed force. To be sure, the pastoral is considering nuclear war, which engenders a very strong version of last resort.

27 O'Brien, *Law and Morality in Israel's War with the PLO*, pp. 173–215.

CHAPTER 11

Strategic Vision for the 1990s: Moving Beyond Containment

Madeleine Albright

At the time she delivered this address to the Dwight D. Eisenhower Centennial Conference at West Point on November 15, 1990, over two years before becoming Permanent Representative of the United States to the United Nations, Dr. Albright was the William H. Donner Research Professor of International Affairs, director of the Women in Foreign Service Program, and a most popular (as voted by the students) teacher of comparative politics at the Georgetown School of Foreign Service, as well as president of the Center for National Policy. As she speculated about the future of U.S. policy on the brink of the twenty-first century, the centennial of Eisenhower's birth stimulated her to organize her thoughts on the subject by comparing the current era, the early 1990s, with his presidential era, the 1950s, when she herself was a college student.

Strategic Vision for the 1990s

Let me begin by drawing some comparisons between the way the United States and the world looked in 1950, when the concept of containment really came into its own, and today. We see a different set of problems in 1990 and are having trouble coming up with a concept around which to organize our foreign policy. Finally, I want to use the "V" word—vision—to try out some new ideas with you.

Let us look at the fifties and the nineties by comparing factors that determine how a nation's foreign policy is formulated. One way to think about the influences on the process is to determine first what a country's objective international position is, then to assess how a country feels about itself. You must look at how the government is organized and what roles various groups inside and outside the government are playing. And finally you should note which individuals are dominating the process.

A Look at the Fifties

Have you noticed the commercials recently? There is a lot of nostalgia about the fifties—small-town coffee shops and gas station attendants who wash your windshields and talk to you. Books on Eisenhower not only talk about his military ability; they also indicate that he was smart and sensitive.

What made the fifties what they were? The United States had come out of World War II the undisputed victor. We had suffered casualties, but our soldiers could come home to rebuild their lives on a rich continent—bordered by two oceans and two unthreatening, basically friendly neighbors. By all objective factors we were the superpower—in both military and economic terms. We were the superior nuclear power and our gross national product was larger than anyone else's.

Madeleine K. Albright

In contrast to the end of World War I, we were both willing and able to act as the linchpin of a new international system. We understood our responsibilities and supplied our friends with funds to rebuild their devastated economies and with arms to defend themselves. By all objective factors we had a right to feel threatened by the presence of the Soviet Union—a massive continental power with major military potential. But we were not paralyzed by the rivalry. In fact we felt more than prepared to deal with what could be a protracted East-West struggle.

The reason for our positive attitude has to do with the second set of factors on which foreign policy decisions are based—that is, how a society feels about itself. The bottom line is that we felt great. As Americans we had a strong positive image of ourselves. We were economically successful in giving our people the highest standard of living in the world. We had a can-do attitude. Nothing could stop Americans.

We believed in democracy for ourselves and saw that other nations in the world respected us. Devastated European nations were grateful for our help. Although they might have found us boorish as tourists, other nations welcomed the almighty dollar. As the great colonial empires started breaking up, their leaders and people looked to us as models.

In the fight with godless communists we were morally superior. Stalin was the face of the enemy, and the North Korean invasion of South Korea gave us a chance to prove our resolve to fight communism. As President Truman told a national radio audience in September 1950, "If aggression were allowed to succeed in Korea, it would be an open invitation to new acts of aggression elsewhere. . . . We cannot hope to maintain our own freedom if freedom elsewhere is wiped out." While Truman committed troops without congressional approval, there was general support for his actions. As time passed, some Americans questioned how much we should sacrifice for others, but few doubted that we were on the right side of history.

The way a government is structured is the third determining factor in foreign policy. In the area that has come to be known as national security, the United States Constitution di-

Strategic Vision for the 1990s

vides power between the executive and legislative branches. When different parties control the two branches the potential for division is even greater. Although the presidency and Congress were in the hands of different political parties during half of the fifties, the executive branch dominated foreign policy. Congress played very much of a supporting role. The defense budget for FY 1951, for example, was a 257 percent increase over the original White House request.[1]

The government structure is not static, however. Foreign policy is affected also by the roles bureaucrats play within the machinery and by the pressures exerted by various interest groups. The fifties saw the beginning of the National Security Council system. Invented by bureaucrats to put some order into the decision-making system after Roosevelt, the NSC began to play its coordinating role during the Korean War. With his military training, Eisenhower used the system to control the rivalries within the bureaucracy that might threaten his and his secretary of state's direction of foreign policy. Various interest groups did function, among them ethnic and ideological ones, such as the China lobby and the McCarthyites, who saw Communists under the beds. Although they made the president uncomfortable, they did not deflect him from his goals.

Finally, individuals if they are strong play a key role in foreign policy-making. In looking back over the fifties, the names stand out—Truman, Marshall, Acheson, McArthur, Eisenhower, Dulles. The views and actions identified with these men are the hallmarks of the national security policy of the fifties.

Undoubtedly one of the reasons for those nostalgic commercials is that, while the fifties were not without problems, everything seemed much simpler. As a college student at the time, I can report to you how we felt: We knew who we were and we knew who our enemy was.

If Paul Nitze, the opening speaker, can rightfully be called one of the fathers of the containment policy, I can be labeled a child of containment. As such, I can assure you that I felt that

---

[1] John Lewis Gaddis, *Strategies of Containment* (Oxford University Press, 1982), p. 113.

Madeleine K. Albright

we were doing absolutely the right thing to fight communism where we could. (I might have felt differently if I had been a male of draft age.) I believed that this was the best country in the world, and having been raised an internationalist, I thought it was absolutely correct for us to play a pivotal part in one regional alliance after another. I was a whiz on the I.D. parts of my exams when we had to identify all that alphabet soup.

Even though I knew that we had lost our nuclear monopoly, that the Soviets had launched Sputnik and had ICBMs, I felt confident we would prevail. After all, I had read Fainsod, Friedrich, Brzezinski, Shapiro, and Kennan, among others. I knew that ultimately a system built on false foundations and that enslaved its people had to fail.

One of our English professors at Wellesley, when I was a student there, had just helped to write the lyrics for Leonard Bernstein's *Candide*. One of the songs based on Voltaire's original included the line "All is for the best in this best of all possible worlds." I must say, that is how my friends and I felt. We were filled with optimism about the United States and the international environment.

And Now the Nineties

I am still an optimist. But the situation in the nineties is quite different from that of the fifties, and I believe the United States has to take quite a different approach to its international responsibilities. Why? Because in asking about the five factors affecting foreign policy decision-making, the answers today are quite different from four decades ago.

First, as to the objective factors, the last time I looked we were still a large continental power behind two oceans. But they do not protect us the way they used to: There are strategic weapons that can reach us, and our people are as worried about cooking from global warming as they are from nuclear weapons. Our neighbors to the north and south are certainly not going to attack us, but they are posing greater economic and social problems for us than in the past.

The second objective difference is that although we continue to be a dominant power, we are no longer the undisputed

Strategic Vision for the 1990s

head of the so-called free world. Others have gained prominence economically, if not militarily. Rather than being the undisputed hegemon, we are the preeminent partner.

The third difference is that the international system itself has changed. Frankly, it is out of kilter. The role of the nation state has diminished, while at the same time nationalism and subnational ethnic rivalries are cropping up. Nonstate actors are playing increasingly important roles. Arms and drug dealers and international businessmen and bankers are taking actions over which no government has control. And what was the U.S.-Soviet rivalry around which all others revolved has now entered a post-Copernican stage. The two superpowers are no longer at the center of everything. And to complicate matters even further one of the superpowers is in the process of disintegrating.

Frankly, while I have no nostalgia for the Cold War, I am willing to argue that the world is actually a much more dangerous place now that the Cold War is over. Just consider that we soon may have a half-million troops in the Persian Gulf area.

The subjective factors in the nineties are also quite different from those in the fifties. The main difference is that we do not feel as good about ourselves as we did then. While our leaders are taking bows for having won the Cold War, we do not feel the way we did after World War II.

We believe that our economy is not the best, that in some ways the Japanese and the Germans are doing better than we are. We cannot solve problems at home and abroad by throwing money at them. We were supposed to get a peace dividend. That bonus was probably never going to be large enough to deal with our many domestic social problems, but we did not plan to spend it so soon on our gasoline bill, a new military buildup, an unprecedented deficit, and a scandalous S&L crisis. In contrast to your parents who finished school in the fifties, many of you cannot expect to earn more than, or for that matter as much as, your parents.

Perhaps the most peculiar reason for not feeling good at this time is that we do not really have a sense of mission. For so many years we could define our role as fighting communism. Since that battle has been won, it has been hard to find as simple an organizing principle for mobilizing the people. Before the Gulf War, President Bush was trying to persuade us that democratization was our goal. Once Saddam Hussein burst on the scene, he became our chosen enemy.

What about the structure of our government? The best verb to describe it in this autumn of 1990 is paralyzed. The natural antagonism of the legislative and executive branches has been exacerbated by the continued control of each branch by opposing parties. Disagreements that cannot be blamed on institutional division can be attributed to partisan wrangling.

One message from the 1990 midterm elections that the pundits have not had trouble picking up is massive voter alienation and party gridlock. With a looming presidential election in the picture for the next two years, there is no reason to expect that the situation in Washington will get any better in 1991 and 1992

A further cause of government ineffectiveness is the increased influence of interest groups within and outside government. At a time of shrinking resources, various departments within the government are competing with each other for funds. Competition among different groups adds to the cacophony of sounds, making it difficult to hear any coherent message.

One of the major problems, I believe, is that our leaders are sounding an uncertain trumpet. As I mentioned at the outset of this analysis, individuals are the final factor in determining the national security policy of a country. At this moment, at the start of the 1990s, there is no one on the scene on either end of Pennsylvania avenue who is giving us a clear definition of our national interest or articulating a policy to take us into the twenty-first century.

Although I am not a kinder, gentler observer of President Bush, I am the first to admit that his task is a difficult one.

Looking Ahead

In your courses you have studied definitions of national interest that, with variations, cover the defense of a nation's people, territory, and way of life. In the past you could do all three by building up your military arsenal and standing tall. With each

Strategic Vision for the 1990s

year, the assignment for this country has become more complicated by the fact that our territory does not extend only from sea to shining sea and from Detroit, Michigan, to Brownsville, Texas, but up into the atmosphere and deep into the ground.

And despite the vastness of our own territory, our people do not stay put. They travel on airlines and cruise ships, they work and study abroad, they tempt fate by living in hostile areas.

Always difficult to define, in the 1990s "our way of life" does not exist in isolation. Our enviable standard of living depends on commerce with others. Our own democratic system is safer in a world populated by other democracies. We believe that our freedom is threatened if a dictatorial bully can invade a neighbor with impunity.

It does not take a rocket scientist to understand that these types of interests cannot be defended by the United States alone, no matter how strong we are militarily. Our territory cannot be protected from global warming and drugs unilaterally; our economic security cannot be guaranteed by closing down our borders to foreign investment and practicing autarky; our peace of mind cannot be guaranteed by turning our backs on the starvation and disease of others.

To protect our national interest in the twenty-first century the United States must have a foreign policy that puts us squarely in a leadership position with partners in a functioning international community. Although it did not get very far in the 1988 campaign, a new concept for how we operate (not ends but means) in the twenty-first century is multilateralism—or partnership, if you like that better—not unilateralism.

Containment was a negative concept. That concept, around which we organized our foreign policy for the last forty years, was based on the idea that we had to contain an evil force and wait for it to change. Let's do better. The new national security agenda needs a positive concept. I'm not sure that this word will ever catch on—I know George Kennan, George Kennan is a friend of mine, and I am no George Kennan—but how about "integration" as a new organizing principle?

We need a concept that will allow us to deal with the more complicated—and frankly more dangerous—world that we are entering. We need a concept that reflects the need to engage with the new democracies, with economically troubled Third World nations, with environmental problems that know no borders, with refugees and nuclear weapons that proliferate.

Open the paper on any given day and you will see what I have started to call "institution bind." Like kids constrained by clothes they have outgrown, nations' aspirations are limited by current institutions: Ask the Lithuanians about the Soviet Union, ask the European Economic Community about its proposal to form a defense community. "Beyond containment" is not good enough. The development of a new world order, which the president has mentioned on occasion, must become a top priority.

Like a bolt of summer lightning that suddenly illuminates the evening landscape, the Iraqi invasion of Kuwait has revealed much about what lies ahead. The brutal act of aggression has not only pointed up how essential it is for us to understand the nature of the new post–Cold War threats to the international system, but also, paradoxically, has provided us with the opportunity to conduct ourselves in a manner that will help build a system to deal with those threats. Broad-based coalitions, multinational sanctions, internationally approved use of force—these will prove to be key tools for dealing with those who threaten their neighbors with weapons of mass destruction.

The hope is that the president—who has so masterfully assembled support from so many nations—will remember that his actions in this situation will set the pattern for conduct in the twenty-first century, and that we do not win when we bomb our enemies into the ground, because we only create new generations of malcontents. We can only win if we work to develop a new international community that works together to discipline those who break its rules. Containment has succeeded—integration is next.

Let me conclude my remarks by putting forward an idea. You may think it is far-fetched. These days all those who propose something that seems off the wall can find a ready response by pointing to any one of the amazing events of the past year, such

Strategic Vision for the 1990s

as the presence of Soviet troops on NATO territory—as in Germany today—in the absence of war.

Twice in this century when major wars have ended, the victors have sat down at conference tables to hammer out a new international order. The end of the Cold War should involve a similar undertaking. We need a new conference that will bring together both nation states and nonstate actors to engage in a dialogue about greater international cooperation, and to agree on a framework that would be effective both in coping with traditional and nontraditional threats to national security and in anticipating the opportunities ahead.

We do not need to be nostalgic about the fifties. What we must do is to keep in mind the factors influencing foreign policy, change those we can, and deal with those we cannot change.

About the Authors

MADELEINE K. ALBRIGHT has served since January 1993 as the Permanent Representative of the United States to the United Nations in New York. At the time of her appointment as ambassador, she was teaching comparative politics and foreign policy at Georgetown and serving as president of the Center for National Policy in Washington, a "think tank" of the National Democratic Institute for International Affairs. Joining Georgetown in 1982 after a year as a fellow at the Smithsonian's Woodrow Wilson International Center for Scholars, she was William H. Donner Research Professor of International Affairs and director of the Women in Foreign Service Program in the Walsh School of Foreign Service. In 1989 she was a regular participant in the television series *Great Decisions '89*, moderated by SFS Dean Peter Krogh.

Dr. Albright served in 1976–78 as senior legislative assistant to Senator Edmund S. Muskie and in 1978–81 on the National Security Council staff at the White House, where she was responsible for foreign policy legislation. In 1984 she was foreign policy advisor to vice presidential candidate Geraldine Ferraro and foreign policy coordinator of the Mondale for President campaign. In 1988 she was senior foreign policy advisor to the Dukakis campaign. She earned her doctorate in public law and government at Columbia University and is the author of *Poland: The Role of the Press in Political Change* (Praeger 1983).

JULES E. DAVIDS, a prolific diplomatic historian, was professor of American history and diplomacy at Georgetown, where he earned MSFS and PhD degrees and taught from 1946 to 1986. During his tenure at Georgetown he spent the year 1964–65 on the staff of the Council on Foreign Relations, for whom he wrote *The United States in World Affairs 1964* (Harper & Row 1965) and coedited *Documents on American Foreign Relations.* Earlier, in 1955, he assisted President (then Senator) John F. Kennedy in the research and writing of *Profiles in Courage.* He was also a visiting professor at the Universidad Iberoamericana in Mexico (summer 1956), at the Johns Hopkins University in Baltimore (1966–67) and Washington (spring 1968), and at the University of Massachusetts (Summer 1968).

Professor Davids made major contributions to the literature of U.S. diplomatic history. In 1970 he established the journal of the Society for Historians of American Foreign Relations, *Diplomatic History.* He edited the three-part, fifty-three-volume series *American Diplomatic and Public Papers: The United States and China* (Scholarly Resources 1973–81), as well as *Perspectives in American Diplomacy: Essays on Europe, Latin America, China, and the Cold War* (Arno Press 1976). In addition to authoring *American Political and Economic Penetration of Mexico, 1877–1920* (Arno Press 1976), he wrote *America and the World of Our Time: United States Diplomacy in the Twentieth Century*, published by Random House in three editions (1960, 1962, 1970).

Frank L. Fadner, S.J. (1910–1987) entered the Society of Jesus in 1933 after graduating from the Georgetown School of Foreign Service, where he later obtained his Master's degree in 1940. After earning licentiates in philosphy and theology at Woodstock College in Maryland, he was ordained a priest in 1943. Father Fadner taught history and languages at the University of Scranton in 1944–46, then studied geopolitics at the University of London, where he earned his doctorate in Russian history in 1949, the year he joined the Georgetown University history faculty.

A close friend and associate of Edmund A. Walsh, founder and regent of the School of Foreign Service, Father Fadner served as executive assistant to the regent from 1950 to 1955, when he succeeded Father Walsh as regent of the School. From 1962 until his retirement in 1978, Father Fadner was regent of the university's School of Languages and Linguistics. He also served as chairman of the Russian Department in 1972. He is the author of *Seventy Years of Pan-Slavism in Russia: Karazin to Danilevskii, 1800–1870* (Georgetown University Press 1962).

WALTER I. (JACK) GILES entered the School of Foreign Service as a freshman in 1938 and, with time out for the U.S. Army Air Force (1945–46), continued his association with Georgetown until he retired from the faculty in 1990. He earned the BSFS (1943), MA (1946), and PhD (1956) degrees at Georgetown and also served as secretary to SFS founder and regent Father Walsh in 1944–50.

Classroom teaching was Professor Giles's central professional interest. He taught numerous courses in comparative government and American government and politics, especially constitutional law and the presidency, from 1947 to 1990 and was active in the movement that led to creating the SFS Core Faculty in 1970. In 1967 he was the first recipient of the annual SFS Senior Class Faculty Award, which cited his "dedication to his students, his profession," the School, and the University. In 1985 he received the GU Alumni's Award for University Service, for "providing the educational experience that engenders alumni loyalty." He also had the distinctive pleasure of hearing a member of the class of 1968, President William J. Clinton—in a 1993 televised interview— cite him as "a terrific teacher."

JAN KARSKI joined the Georgetown School of Foreign Service faculty in 1949. He taught courses in government and international affairs from 1952 until retiring in 1984, since which time he has continued to teach as adjunct professor of national security studies. He holds MA degrees in both law and diplomatic science from his native Poland and a doctorate in international relations from Georgetown and is the author of various articles and studies on East European affairs. His book *Story of a Secret State* (Houghton Mifflin 1944) was the December 1944 Book of the Month Club selection and was published in Paris (Editions S.E.L.F. 1948) as *Mon témoignage devant le monde (Histoire d'un état secret)*. In 1985 University Press of America published his major scholarly work, *The Great Powers and Poland, 1919–1945: From Versailles to Yalta*.

For over three decades Dr. Karski lectured intensively for academic and civic organizations and government agencies, including two six-month lecture tours to Asia and Francophone Africa for the U.S. Department of State. He was awarded the Order *Virtuti Militari*, Poland's highest military decoration, for his activities during and after World War II, including his eyewitness report on the besieged Warsaw ghetto, which he delivered in person to President Roosevelt and Justice Frankfurter. A tree bearing the name of Jan Karski was planted in Jerusalem in the Alley of the Righteous Gentiles among the Nations. Georgetown University awarded him a degree of Doctor of Humane Letters, *honoris causa*.

WILLIAM V. O'BRIEN is an expert on war, morality, and the legal dimensions of international affairs. Interrupting his undergraduate education at Georgetown to serve in the U.S. Army in 1943–46, he returned after the war, earning BSFS, MSFS, and PhD (1953) degrees and taught international law and relations at Georgetown from 1950 until his retirement in 1993. He twice chaired the government department (1974–77, 1983–84), founded and directed its Goldman Visiting Israeli Professor Program, and received a GU doctorate of humane letters, *honoris causa*, in 1992. The department and the School of Foreign Service, on whose curriculum he left an indelible stamp, honored his distinguished service to the university by establishing a biennial lectureship in his name when he retired. An officer for nearly 25 years in the Army Reserve, often assigned at the Pentagon, he served as consulting faculty at the Army's Command and General Staff College at Fort Leavenworth and its War College at Carlisle.

Dr. O'Brien has also been active in Catholic organizations concerned with international moral issues, most notably as an advisor to the American Catholic Bishops on morality and strategic nuclear deterrence. He is the author of *The Conduct of Just and Limited War* (Praeger 1981), *Law and Morality in Israel's War with the PLO* (Routledge 1991), and five other books, and contributor/coeditor of *The Nuclear Dilemma and the Just War Tradition* (Lexington 1986) and *The New Nations in International Law and Diplomacy* (Praeger/Stevens 1965), among others. He is also the author of numerous chapters in other books and encyclopedias and dozens of articles in law reviews and scholarly and religious journals.

CARROLL QUIGLEY (1910–1977), a pioneer world system theorist and comparative civilizationist known for his unconventional and creative intellect and wide interdisciplinary interests, taught at Georgetown from 1941 to 1976. Earlier, he had taught briefly at Princeton and at Harvard, where he studied under Crane Brinton and earned his BA, MA, and PhD (1938) degrees. From 1941 to 1969 the School of Foreign Service alumni cited his Development of Civilization course as the most influential course in their undergraduate studies. In 1964 he received the university's 175th anniversary Medal of Merit. In the 1950s Professor Quigley was a consultant to the Defense Department, the Navy, and the House Select Committee on Astronautics and Space Exploration. He also advised the Smithsonian on the layout of the American History section of its new Museum of History and Technology.

His major theoretical work, *The Evolution of Civilizations: An Introduction to Historical Analysis* (Macmillan 1961; 2nd ed., Liberty Press 1979), was also published in Brazil (Funda de Cultura 1963) and Mexico (Hermés 1963). Other works included his monumental *Tragedy and Hope: A History of the World in Our Time* (Macmillan 1966), Part II of which was republished as *The World since 1939: A History* (Collier 1968), and three posthumous publications—the 1976 Oscar Iden Lectures, *Public Authority and the State in the Western Tradition: A Thousand Years of Growth, 976–1976* (Georgetown School of Foreign Service 1977); *The Anglo-American Establishment: From Rhodes to Cliveden* (Books in Focus 1981); and *Weapons Systems and Political Stability: A History* (University Press of America 1983).

JOSEPH S. SEBES, S.J. (1915–1990), a native of Hungary, came to Georgetown in 1958 from Harvard, where he earned a doctorate in history and Far Eastern languages under John Fairbank. Earlier, after earning his licentiate in philosophy in Budapest, he had entered the Society of Jesus in 1934 and spent the following years in China, where he was ordained in 1946. The Jesuit Historical Institute in Rome then called upon him to edit the "Monumenta Sinica," a collection of documents on the Jesuit mission in China in the 16th to 18th centuries, a project interrupted by his studies at the Gregorianum, where he earned a licentiate in history and missiology before heading for Harvard and thence to Georgetown. His book *The Jesuits and the Sino-Soviet Treaty of Nerchinsk, 1689* (Institutum Historicum S.I. 1961) was said to have made an important contribution to Chinese border claims.

From 1958 until 1976, Father Sebes contributed to Georgetown as teacher, scholar, administrator, and fund-raiser. While carrying a full teaching schedule, he also served as regent of the Foreign Service and Business Administration schools, representing both schools on the university's board of trustees (1961–64); as acting dean of the Business School (1964–66); and as SFS dean (1966–68). He developed the graduate program in East Asian history and received an honorary Georgetown degree for his singular service. In 1976–77 he was a Woodrow Wilson scholar at the Smithsonian. Finally, in 1984, he returned to Rome to resume editing the "Monumenta Sinica" series, the work he had begun in 1947 and in which he remained immersed until his death.

GEORGE J. VIKSNINS is professor of economics at Georgetown, where he has taught since earning his doctorate there (as H.B. Earhart Fellow) in 1964. He has directed both graduate and undergraduate economic studies and, since 1983, has directed the Institute for Comparative Political and Economic Systems. He is an expert on taxation and regulation of financial institutions and on the economies of Asia and the Baltic states, on which he has written, spoken, and consulted widely through congressional testimony, academic and professional conference papers, and participation in panels and symposia in the United States and abroad. He has authored *The Economies of Southeast Asia in the 1980s* (Center for Strategic and International Studies 1975) and *Financial Deepening in the ASEAN Countries* (University of Hawaii Press 1980); coauthored *Financing East Asia's Success* (Macmillan 1987); coedited *The Economic and Political Growth Pattern of Asia-Pacific* (Pacific Forum 1976); and published numerous articles in *Intereconomics*, *Journal of Finance*, *Asian Survey*, *Banking*, and *Journal of Baltic Studies*.

Dr. Viksnins was program economist at the USAID mission in Bangkok (1968–70), made three overseas lecture tours for the U.S. Information Agency, and has been a consultant to other federal agencies, the World Bank, the Federal Reserve Board of Governors, and private foundations and think tanks. He was chairman of the Baltic Studies Fund in 1983–89 and since August 1992 has been senior advisor to the Bank of Latvia.

EDMUND A. WALSH, S.J. (1885–1956) founded the Georgetown University School of Foreign Service in 1919 at the age of thirty-four. As its regent until 1955, he directed its development into a nationally recognized, unique institution of higher learning. He entered the Society of Jesus in 1902, studied at Woodstock College in Maryland, earned a BA at Georgetown (1909), studied in Dublin, London, and Innsbruck, and was ordained (1916) and earned an MA (1917) at Woodstock. As an innovative educator, serious student of the Russian Revolution, and analyst of the Soviet system, Father Walsh became an influential, at times controversial, national figure, with a reputation as an authoritative scholar. He served in Soviet Russia as director-general of the Papal Relief Mission and Vatican representative for church interests (1922–23), in Washington as organizer of the Finnish Relief Fund (1939–40), and in Nuremberg as consultant to Justice Robert H. Jackson (1945–46).

Father Walsh was an exceptionally prolific writer of books and articles and a frequent public speaker. Among his principal books were *The Fall of the Russian Empire: The Story of the Last Romanovs and the Coming of the Bolsheviki* (Little Brown 1928); *The Last Stand: An Interpretation of the Soviet Five-Year Plan* (Little Brown 1931); *Ships and National Safety* (Georgetown School of Foreign Service 1934); *The Woodcarver of Tyrol* (Harper & Brothers 1935); *Total Power: A Footnote to History* (Doubleday 1948); and *Total Empire: The Roots and Progress of World Communism* (Bruce 1951, also published in Italian in Milan). In 1989 Georgetown University Press published a selection of Father Walsh's numerous speeches and writings, *Footnotes to History*, edited by Anna Watkins with an introduction by Walter I. Giles, from which this portrait has been drawn.

Joseph Zrinyi, S.J. (1919–1991) descended from prominent Hungarian patriots and writers of the 15th and 16th centuries. Entering the Jesuit Novitiate in Budapest in 1937, he specialized in languages and sacred eloquence. In 1943 he obtained his licentiate in philosophy in what was then Kassa in northern Hungary. During the war he was associate editor of two Budapest Jesuit magazines, then taught at a seminary in Eastern Hungary. He had to break off his theological studies in Szeged because of the Communist suppression of the seminaries and instead completed his licentiate in theology in the Netherlands at Maastricht in 1949. After a year in Belgium he began serving as a priest in Canada and earned his MA in industrial relations from the University of Montreal in 1953.

Moving to the United States that same year, Father Zrinyi served with the Hungarian Province in Exile, led retreats and missions to U.S. and Canadian Hungarian communities, and edited the Hungarian edition of the *Messenger of the Sacred Heart*. He came to Georgetown in 1958, earned his PhD in economics in 1962, and served on the economics faculty from 1961 until retiring in 1989, having been repeatedly voted outstanding teacher by his undergraduate students in basic economics. His writings included essays on mercantilism and the physiocrats in *The New Catholic Encyclopedia*, a contribution "The Changing Status of Unionism" in a Festschrift for Goetz A. Briefs, and articles on entrepreneurial behavior in economic theory.

MARGERY BOICHEL THOMPSON is director of publications and editor of the Georgetown School of Foreign Service Institute for the Study of Diplomacy, which she joined in 1980. She was coeditor and compiler (with Smith Simpson) of *Education in Diplomacy: An Instructional Guide* (ISD/University Press of America 1987) and editor of *As Others See Us: United States Diplomacy Viewed from Abroad* (ISD 1989) and has collaborated with ISD authors and publishers in the development, editing, and publication of many other ISD books, reports, and monographs. Her previous appointments have included the Institute of International Education, the Brookings Institution, the University of Pittsburgh Center for Regional Economic Studies, and the Pittsburgh Commission on Human Relations. She was educated at Northwestern University, the University of Pittsburgh, and George Washington University.